ABOUT THE AUTHOR . . .

ARTHUR SKEVINGTON WOOD represents the Movement for World Evangelization. Born at Ashbourne, Derbyshire, England, he took his early schooling there, went on to Wesley College, Headingley and later received his degree in Theology from the University of London. Dr. Wood, a Fellow of the Royal Historical Society, was closely associated with the Billy Graham "Tell Scotland" movement and is well known as a preacher, broadcaster, convention speaker and writer. He is the author of a number of books, the most recent of which is *Prophecy in the Space Age,* published in 1963.

Dr. Wood received his Ph.D. degree from the University of Edinburgh.

Life by the Spirit

Life by the Spirit

(Formerly published as Paul's Pentecost*)*

by
A. SKEVINGTON WOOD
B.A., Ph.D., Fr. Hist. S.

ZONDERVAN PUBLISHING HOUSE
Grand Rapids, Michigan

Originally published under the title *Paul's Pentecost:
Studies in the Life of the Spirit from Romans 8.*
This American edition under the title *Life by the Spirit*
is published by arrangement with The Paternoster Press.

Printed in the United States of America

CONTENTS

CONTENTS

CHAPTER ONE

THE THEME OF THE SPIRIT

ONE HUNDRED YEARS AGO there was no more fascinating
and compulsive figure on the Scottish scene than
George Wilson. His charm of personality, his enquiring
mind, his lightning wit and his exceptional powers of
expression justified the claims of his contemporaries that
he was to be classified as a genius. Scientific investigator,
educational reformer, felicitous biographer, no mean poet,
he shone as a light in a dark place. "Indeed," according
to Dr. Alexander R. McEwen, "no more beautiful or
brilliant character flashed upon the monotony which
ecclesiasticism and medicine imparted to Scottish thought
in the middle of the century."

Above all these things, Wilson was a Christian. God
spoke to him through a crippling illness. Up to this point,
so his friend and spiritual counsellor, Dr. John Cairns,
tells us, "his great want was the power to realize the value
of the Gospel remedy, from his heart having been greatly
set on literary and scientific eminence." But face to face
with death he was impressed with the same word of
chastening and rebuke which came to Baruch the scribe:
"And do you seek great things for yourself? Seek them
not" (Jer. 45:5). Under the wise and tender guidance of
the earnest Cairns, George Wilson gained a clear faith in
God and a firm assurance of salvation which never left him.
He also found a new zest for Bible reading and, though
pain was to be his constant companion, he drew strength
to endure from the well of God's Word. He made a special
study of Paul's letter to the Romans and reported progress
to Cairns. "You have got far in reading Romans with

7

genuine interest," the latter replied. "The Gospel tide
nowhere forms so many deep, dark pools where the neo-
phyte may drown . . . You will have something like a
glimpse of the divine depth and richness of that despised
old text-book, the New Testament."

Cairns evidently concurred with the verdict of Coleridge
that Romans is the most profound work in existence, and
such in fact is the immediate impression created by this
most weighty of all Paul's writings. But as we proceed to
open its pages with perhaps trembling fingers at the outset
of this series of expositions, let us not be misled into supposing that it is too complicated to bring profit to simple
believers. Every portion of God's Word affords blessing
and enlightenment to those who read in faith and although
Paul's major epistle handles themes both deep and high,
it can yet speak to the need of the latest babe in Christ
who allows the Interpreter Spirit to make plain God's
eternal truth.

The Roman letter contains an epitome of evangelical
doctrine and it is significant that in every period of
evangelical renascence it has figured prominently. By
accepted tradition, four great names are now recognized
as representing the evangelical succession, which we
would claim to be a true apostolical succession as well.
The line opens with Paul himself and leads through Augustine and Luther to John Wesley. How remarkable it is
that the epistle to the Romans links them all! Paul, of
course, was its author and in it he gave his evangelical
testimony: "I am not ashamed of the gospel: it is the
power of God for salvation to every one who has faith,
to the Jew first and also to the Greek. For in it the righteousness of God is revealed through faith for faith; as it is
written, 'He who through faith is righteous shall live'."
(1:16, 17).

Romans was used by God to effect the conversion of the
mighty Augustine. As a headstrong youth who had left
his North African home for the pleasures of Italy, much
to the distress of his mother Monica, he was arrested by

this very portion of God's Book. After a conversation with a Christian friend, he resorted to a quiet garden where he might think and pray things through. He was keenly conscious of his divided self. The good that he wanted he could not do and the evil that he did not want he found himself continually doing. His will was maimed and struggling, "with one part sinking as another arose." As he was thus torn in spirit and weeping in bitter contrition of heart, he heard from a neighbouring house a child's voice – whether it was a boy or a girl he could not tell – singing again and again *"Tolle, lege"* – "Take up, and read." Apparently it was a snatch of some ditty or perhaps part of a nursery game. But to Augustine it came as the command of God Himself. He hurried into the house, opened his Bible and read these words from the epistle to the Romans: "Let us conduct ourselves becomingly as in the day, not in reveling and drunkenness, not in debauchery and licentiousness, not in quarreling and jealousy. But put on the Lord Jesus Christ, and make no provision for the flesh, to gratify its desires" (13:13,14). "No further would I read," he tells us, in his *Confessions*, "nor needed I; for instantly at the end of this sentence, by a light as it were of serenity infused into my heart, all the darkness of doubt vanished away." Augustine found salvation in Christ through reading in Romans – and the Church was braced to endure the mortal storm when the city of Rome fell.

The centuries pass: the fashion of this world changes, and we are brought to the brink of modern times. The uncertain twilight of the Middle Ages was yielding to the dawn of a glorious new day. A German born monk sat in his cell high up in the Black Tower of the Augustinian monastery at Wittenberg. His name was Martin Luther and he was questing after a gracious God and the way of life. He found it there as he pondered the Divine Word in Paul's epistle to the Romans. His eye fell upon the seventeenth verse of the opening chapter and in a flash the eternal truth was borne in upon him. "At last," he

informs us, "God being merciful, as I meditated day and
night on the connexion of the words, namely 'for in it the
righteousness of God is revealed through faith for faith;
as it is written, He who through faith is righteous shall
live,' there I began to understand the righteousness of
God as that by which the just lives by the gift of God,
namely, by faith, and this sentence 'in it the righteousness
of God is revealed' to be that passive righteousness by
which God justifies us by faith, as it is written 'The righteous
shall live by faith.' This straightway made me feel as if
reborn, and as though I had entered through open gates
into paradise itself. From then on, the whole face of
Scripture appeared different . . . And now, as much as
I had hated this word 'righteousness of God' before, so
much the more sweetly I extolled this word to myself
now, so that this place was to me a real gate of paradise."
Martin Luther found saving faith through reading in
Romans – and the Reformation was born.

Once more the pages of history turn and we are brought
to the ever-memorable evening of May 24, 1738. A young
Anglican clergyman in much distress of soul went very
unwillingly, like Shakspere to school, to a predominantly
Moravian society meeting in Aldersgate Street, London.
There someone (probably William Holland) was reading
from Luther's preface to Romans. "About a quarter
before nine," records John Wesley in his *Journal* – for
he it was on whom God's hand was to be laid – "while
he was describing the change which God works in the
heart through faith in Christ, I felt my heart strangely
warmed. I felt I did trust in Christ, Christ alone for my
salvation; and an assurance was given me that He had
taken away my sins, even *mine*, and saved *me* from the
law of sin and death." Dr. Henry Bett succeeded in tracing
the precise passage from Luther's introduction to Romans
which must have so warmed Wesley's heart. Here is
how it runs "Wherefore let us conclude that faith alone
justifies, and that faith alone fulfils the law. For faith
through the merit of Christ obtains the Holy Spirit, which

Spirit makes us new hearts, exhilarates, excites and influences our heart, so that it may do those things willingly of love, which the law commands; and so, at the last, good works indeed proceed from the faith which works so mightily, and which is so lively in our hearts." Thus John Wesley was converted by reading in Romans – and the Evangelical Revival was inaugurated.

We may therefore feel justified in supposing that a volume in the sacred library which has been so signally associated with spiritual quickening in the past is likely to repay our close consideration today and may once again be used in the merciful providence of God to awaken His people from slumber.

Our concern in this set of expositions, however, is not with the letter in its entirety. We propose to focus attention upon a single chapter – that which speaks most prolifically of the Holy Spirit. It is with the Pentecost of Romans that we shall be occupied and we find it in the eighth chapter. Professor William Sanday called this "the second climax" of the epistle, and Matthew Arnold in his *St. Paul and Protestantism* listed it as one of the two primary sections, along with Chapter Six. Writing of this same remarkable passage, Dr. David Brown has said that "within this space some of the richest matter, dear to Christian experience, is compressed; and as almost every verse in this portion opens up some fresh view of the Spirit's work, the light which it throws upon this vital department of the work of redemption is out of all proportion to the space which it fills."

Returning to Sanday's phrase, we shall find the first climax of Romans in Chapter Five, which brings the teaching on justification to a head. Chapter Eight similarly brings the teaching on sanctification to a head. It is the climax, moreover, not only of this particular section from Chapter Six onwards, but also of the whole epistle. It represents the peak-point of Romans. After the parenthetical treatment of election in Chapters Nine to Eleven (or what Dr. Thiessen calls the dispensational harmonization), the practical application from 12:1 to 15:13 is a direct outcome of what has been taught concerning the Spirit in Chapter Eight. The boundless possibilities of the Pentecostal life flow out into the concluding section of the epistle.

It is the distinctive emphasis laid upon the work of the Holy Spirit which marks off this chapter from the rest. It is indeed the Pentecost of Romans. The Spirit is mentioned no less than nineteen times in the space of thirty-nine verses. As Agar Beet observed, "The Spirit is the new and conspicuous feature of Chapter Eight." It is, then, with a view to quickening our own spiritual life that we propose to resort to this dynamic sector of the Word. We shall prove the truth of what James Gilmour, the missionary to Mongolia, once said about it. "Romans Eight," he wrote, "I find good reading in dull spiritual weather." If dark clouds have obscured the sky and we are feeling at all depressed in soul, this vital chapter will provide an admirable tonic.

Before we plunge into the chapter of our choice, however, we must briefly review the references to the Holy Spirit in the earlier part of Romans. We shall better understand the concentrated message of Chapter Eight when we have considered the scattered allusions which precede it.

Bengel was probably right in claiming that Romans 5:5 represents the first unambiguous mention of the Spirit in this epistle. Some commentators see a reference in 1:4 where we are told that our Lord Jesus Christ was "designated Son of God in power according to the Spirit of holiness by his resurrection from the dead." The capitalization in the Revised Standard Version indicates that the translators took that viewpoint, following Moffatt and Weymouth amongst others. It would appear, nevertheless, that what is intended here is Christ's own spirit, as contrasted with "the flesh" in the third verse. The New English Bible ingeniously combines both possibilities by rendering the phrase as "on the level of the spirit – the Holy Spirit."

The purpose of Paul's epistle is stated in verse eleven of this opening chapter: "that I may impart to you some spiritual gift to strengthen you." Since his visit to Rome is likely to be delayed, Paul hopes to convey his present to the Christians there through the medium of a letter. And what he seeks to pass on to them is a gift of the Spirit – something he himself has received by the Spirit and which he is desirous of sharing with them. Its purpose is to establish them in the faith, that both he and they may be mutually encouraged. But this, of course, is not a direct mention of the Holy Spirit.

We have to wait until the Fifth Chapter for this, at the fifth verse. Here is something to underline in our Bible, for it is one of the key statements of Scripture. "God's love has been poured into our hearts through the Holy Spirit which has been given to us." Or, as A. S. Way vividly paraphrases it, "the brimming river of God's love has already overflowed into our hearts, on-drawn by His Holy Spirit, which He has given to us." This comes at the end of the great argument which shows that justification depends on faith so that the promise may rest on grace (cf.4:16). Since it is by faith that we are made right with God, the apostle says, "let us grasp the fact that we *have* peace with God through our Lord Jesus Christ. Through Him we have confidently entered into this new relationship of grace, and here we take our stand, in the happy certainty of the glorious things He has for us in the future" (5:1,2 Phillips).

But as justified believers we have something more than a blessed hope: we have a present experience. Already the love of God floods our inmost hearts, and this is through the gift of the Holy Spirit. Because of the Spirit, the love of God is something more than a doctrine: it is an actual fact of our inner life. As such it becomes the dominant motive of all our conduct. "We love, because he first loved us" (I John 4:19). Our love to others flows from His love to us. This is the very heart of holiness. It is perfect love. It is our response and reaction to the perfect love of

God. And yet it is not our achievement at all. It is given to us in the Holy Spirit.

The abundance and immeasurability of God's love is suggested by the verb used here. It is poured out. The metaphor harks back to the prophecy of Isaiah. "For I will *pour* water on the thirsty land, and streams on the dry ground; I will *pour* my Spirit upon your descendants, and my blessing on your offspring" (44:3). The same word recurs in Acts 2 to describe the outpouring of Pentecost. Verse seventeen repeats the prophecy of Joel: "And in the last days it shall be, God declares, that I will *pour out* my Spirit upon all flesh." Verse thirty-three records Peter's own description of the phenomenal event: "(This Jesus) being therefore exalted at the right hand of God, and having received from the Father the promise of the Holy Spirit, he has *poured out* this which you see and hear." The identical word is employed when the Spirit is bestowed upon the Gentiles after Peter's sermon in the house of Cornelius. "While Peter was still saying this, the Holy Spirit fell on all who heard the word. And the believers from among the circumcised who came with Peter were amazed, because the gift of the Holy Spirit had been *poured out* even on the Gentiles" (Acts 10:44,45). And in Titus 3:6 it is again associated with the love of God as here in Romans 5:5, for we read of the goodness and loving-kindness of God our Saviour which appeared in Christ and was "*poured out* upon us richly" in the Holy Spirit.

We are taught two most important things, then, in this verse from Romans Five. We learn that the Holy Spirit is a gift. We learn also that through the gift of the Spirit the love of God is poured into the hearts of believers. Or, as Hofmann put it: "The Holy Spirit, who is the effectual cause of holiness of life, was not in us by nature. But now, through Him, the love of God is in our hearts."

Another major reference to the Holy Spirit occurs in Romans 7:6. Paul is contrasting the old life of the flesh with the new life in Christ. When we were in the flesh, he says, the law stimulated our sinful passions and so worked in our nature that we became producers of death. But now we stand clear of the law and are free to serve God not in the old obedience to the letter of the law, but in a totally new way in the Spirit. "We serve not under the old written code, but in the new life of the Spirit." There is an illuminating antithesis here between the new, live, active Spirit of the Gospel as over against the old, dead, formal letter of the law. Henceforward the believer is subject not to an external word of command but to the inner compulsion of the indwelling Spirit. So Pentecost supersedes Sinai. The rule of God is "written not with ink but with the Spirit of the living God, not on tablets of stone but on tablets of human hearts" (II Cor. 3:3), "for the written code kills, but the Spirit gives life" (II Cor. 3:6).

Here is a challenging indication that it is to new life that Christ has called us. "Not to some new steps in life," declares Horatius Bonar, at the outset of his classic, *God's Way of Holiness*, "some new habits or ways or motives or prospects, but to a new life . . . It is not merely the old life retouched and made more comely; defects struck out, roughness smoothed down, graces stuck on here and there. It is not a broken column repaired, a soiled picture cleaned, a defaced inscription filled up, an unswept temple whitewashed. It is more than all this: else God would not call it a *new creation*, nor would the Lord Jesus Christ have affirmed with such awful explicitness, as He does, in His conference with Nicodemus, the Divine Law of exclusion from and entrance into the Kingdom of God (John 3:3). Yet how few in our day believe that 'that which is born of the flesh is flesh, and that which is born of the Spirit is spirit' (John 3:6)."

Go through the New Testament Scriptures and count up the passages which speak of the new life in Christ by the Spirit. Everything begins with the new birth and it unfolds itself in the newness of the Spirit. Believers are "a new creation" (II Cor. 5:17; Gal. 6:15), "newborn babes" (I Pet. 2:2) constituting "a new lump" (A.V.), or "fresh dough" in which the old leaven has been purged out by the Passover sacrifice of Christ (I Cor. 5:7). They grow into a "new man" (Eph. 2:15) with "the new nature" (Eph. 4:24; Col. 3:10), obeying "a new commandment" (John 13:34; I John 3:8), heirs of "a new name" (Rev. 2:17; 3:12), waiting for "new heavens and a new earth" (II Pet. 3:13; Rev. 21:1). This life is lived under "a new covenant" (Heb. 8:8; 9:15), proceeds along "the new and living way" (Heb. 10:20) and leads to "a new song" (Rev. 5:9) in "the new Jerusalem" (Rev. 3:12; 21:3). Let us then rejoice in the glorious newness of this life in the Spirit!

This is the last allusion to the Holy Spirit before we reach the Pentecost of Romans in the next chapter. We shall do well to dwell upon it, for, as Dr. C. H. Dodd points out, "this idea will be magnificently developed in Chapter Eight." But it is not enough merely to meditate upon it. We must seek to make it our own. It was the poet Keats who insisted that "nothing ever becomes real until it is experienced." This teaching about the Holy Spirit pouring the love of God into our hearts and leading us into newness of life will only become real to us as it ceases to be a theory and begins to be an experience. May the gracious work commence even as we "receive with meekness the implanted word" (Jas. 1:21).

CHAPTER TWO

THE LAW OF THE SPIRIT

ONE OF THE OUTSTANDING LEADERS of the Protestant Reformation was Philip Melanchthon. He was the friend and theological adviser of Martin Luther. His tidy mind was responsible for some of the earliest formularies of the rediscovered faith. Professor Wilhelm Pauck names him, along with Calvin and Bucer, as the spokesman of unitive Protestantism.

On the last day of his life, whilst he lay in extreme weakness, Melanchthon opened his eyes after a prolonged silence, and said to his son-in-law, "I have been in death, but God has greatly delivered me." As he repeated the words several times over, his friends felt that he must have been passing through some inward conflict. One of them appropriately began to read to him from Paul's epistle to the Romans. He turned to the eighth chapter and the opening words proved an inexpressible comfort to the dying reformer. His eyes brightened at the assurances, and he responded with some verses from the end of I Cor. 1: "He is the source of your life in Christ Jesus, whom God made our wisdom, our righteousness and sanctification and redemption; therefore, as it is written, 'Let him who boasts, boast of the Lord'." (I Cor. 1:30,31). Then, often reiterating the plea, "Lord, have mercy on me," he prepared himself to meet the end of his earthly pilgrimage.

It is to this vital and vitalising chapter that we are now to turn. As Anders Nygren explains in his exceptionally stimulating commentary on Romans, from the fifth chapter onwards Paul is dealing with the freedom of a Christian man. Prior to that he has shown how necessary

17

it was for both Jew and Gentile to be redeemed from bondage and what means God in His everlasting mercy devised in order to secure such release. In Chapter Five Paul speaks of the Christian's freedom from wrath and attributes it to the love of God. In Chapter Six he speaks of the Christian's freedom from sin and attributes it to the death of Christ. In Chapter Seven he speaks of the Christian's freedom from law and attributes it to the triumph of Christ. In Chapter Eight he speaks of the Christian's freedom from death and attributes it to the Holy Spirit.

The apostle, of course, is alluding to spiritual death as well as to physical. The Christian is indeed delivered from the fear of the grave, but that is the least of his privileges. He is rescued from spiritual destruction and thus need not be afraid of judgement and the second death. Put positively, then, the theme of this climactic chapter of Romans is life: what Henry Scougal, that saintly Scotsman of the seventeenth century whose writings so markedly influenced the Wesleys and Whitefield, called in a memorable phrase "the life of God in the soul of man." Concerning this eighth of Romans, Sanday and Headlam say in their standard text-book on this epistle that "it describes the innermost circle of the Christian life from its beginning to its end – that life of which the Apostle speaks elsewhere as 'hid with Christ in God' (Col. 3:3)."

This chapter, then, has to do with the very best and highest life there is – namely, spiritual life. And as we might deduce from the adjective itself, spiritual life is life by the Spirit. It is the life that stems from Pentecost. It is fed from the source. It is maintained from the spring. It is life *from* the Father, *in* the Son and *through* the Spirit. It is life that is life indeed. Let us then place this overall title at the head of our chosen chapter – *LIFE BY THE SPIRIT*.

Each of the subsections we aim to examine in the course of these studies has to do with some aspect of this life by the Spirit. And the first, to which we must now address ourselves, covers the opening four verses and concerns the law of the Spirit. Each verse is a separate entity and refers to a different aspect of the believer's enablement through the Spirit. Paul both speaks for himself and for every Christian who is drawing upon the fulness of God's provision in the Third Person of the blessed Trinity.

I.   There is first THE CONDEMNATION HE IS ENABLED TO ESCAPE (v.1). This has to do with the believer's exoneration. The chapter starts with a "therefore." The particle always has a backward pointing arrow running through it. There is a reference to something that has already been said, not necessarily immediately beforehand, upon which a further argument is about to be based. The sense is, "In view of what has been stated previously, we can now declare . . ." The New English Bible hits it off well with "The conclusion of the matter is this . . ."

In this instance it could be claimed that what follows in Chapter Eight is a natural consequence of the triumphant affirmation of 7:25. Paul has enquired who can deliver from the body of death, to which he is tied like a prisoner to his guard. "Thanks be to God," he cries (it is surely a shout of victory here) "through Jesus Christ our Lord!" It is perfectly true that the eighth chapter is an outworking of that paean of rejoicing.

But there is another verse further back in Chapter Seven which affords an even more explicit link. Verses 7–25 really form a separate section – a kind of parenthesis dealing with sin and law in the experience of the believer before he has entered into the full life of the Spirit. It is cast in the first person singular and, as we shall have cause to notice later, reflects Paul's own condition. The keyword is "carnal" in v.14 which the New English Bible effectively renders as "unspiritual." We might even write it as "*unSpiritual*" – lacking the completion of the Holy Spirit. If we then regard 7–25 as an autobiographical interlude, we are taken behind it to v.6 as representing Paul's conclusion as he has dealt with the Christian's freedom from law. Here is the firmer point of contact

with v.1 of Chapter Eight. "Now" is the tie that binds
them. "But *now* we are discharged from the law" (7:6).
"There is therefore *now* no condemnation for those who
are in Christ Jesus" (8:1). Moreover, the reference in
7:6 to the new life of the Spirit is a direct introduction
to the theme of Chapter Eight. Romans 7:6 is not only
the end of one paragraph: it is the beginning of another.

Christianity is the religion of "now". To be sure, it
has its roots in history – in the "then" – but it is essentially
a word for "now". That is what makes it so challenging.
It offers life by the Spirit "now": it wants to know why
we are not living by the Spirit "now": and it says that
by faith we can receive that life "now". One of Samuel
Chadwick's students at Cliff College was having rather
a rough time with a paper on Christian doctrine in the
examination room. He was uncomfortably aware of his
shortcomings and so when he had done his best, which
he feared would not be sufficient to satisfy his mentors,
he wrote at the foot of the last page these appealing words:
"Sir, I may not know much about theology, but I know
a lot about 'nowology'." Certainly the theology of the
Bible is 'nowology' too and it would not be difficult to
supply a catena of "nows" from the Word of God in the
same way as we picked out the "news" in our introductory
chapter. Life by the Spirit, then, is not for tomorrow,
but for today: not only for the next world, but for this.
It is "now".

The first feature of this "now" life in the Spirit which
Paul selects for notice is the incredible fact that the believer
is clear of condemnation. This arises from his freedom
with respect to the law. It is the law which brings doom,
but if the Christian is delivered from bondage to the law
by faith in Christ, he no longer comes under the hammer
of its reproof. No verdict of "Guilty" can be passed upon
him now. Not a single charge can be preferred against
him. Paul has already implied this in 5:16,18 – "For the
judgment following one trespass brought condemnation,
but the free gift following many trespasses brings justifi-

cation . . . Then as one man's trespass led to condemnation for all men, so one man's act of righteousness leads
to acquittal and life for all men."

It is by no means suggested, of course, that believers
never fall again into sin or are no longer deserving of
God's just discipline. We are still unworthy sinners and
could not complain if God chose to punish: instead,
He looks at Christ's righteousness and deems it ours since
we are in Him. Nor does this release from condemnation
imply that we can ignore altogether the demands of the
law. As we shall see in v.4, the just requirements of the
law are to be fulfilled in us. But it does mean that no one
can lay anything to the charge of God's elect – not even
the Accuser of the brethren himself. Complete exoneration
is ours.

> *No condemnation now I dread;*
> *Jesus, and all in Him, is mine!*

The rest of the verse defines precisely who are the favoured
reprievees who thus escape the doom of law. We must
not claim the privilege unless we are sure that the conditions
have been met. It is "for those who are in Christ Jesus."
Union with Him is basic. Only those are clear of condemnation who abide in the Vine.

II.   Paul speaks even more personally in the next verse
of THE LIBERATION HE IS ENABLED TO ENJOY (v.2). This
has to do with the believer's emancipation. The apostle
is plainly giving his testimony. He reverts to the autobiographical strain of the previous chapter. In v.1 it is
"those:" here it is "me." In v.4 it is "us." What we have
in v.2 is obviously a personal experience. Paul is telling us
what happened to him. "This is Paul's cry of triumph,"
declared the distinguished American preacher Phillips
Brooks, "over the greatest emancipation of his life."
He discerns three factors in his spiritual encounter.

The first is *the liberating law*. Immediately we are confronted with a paradox. For Paul has just been saying

that a Christian is free from the law. "Of all the stars which fell to earth in the mighty firmament-shaking experience of Paul's conversion," affirmed H. J. Holtzmann, "the law was the greatest." But it is of a quite different law that the apostle speaks here. His deliverance has been effected by the application of another law – "the law of the Spirit of life in Christ Jesus." That is a remarkable and perhaps puzzling feature of Paul's experience. He found that only law can liberate from law. He did not cast off restraint when he came to Christ. He submitted to a new law.

But in this context, law means not so much a set of rules as a regulative principle. Formerly Paul was under the dominion of sin and death. He discovered that only a more powerful dominion, namely that of the Spirit of life in Christ Jesus, could snap his fetters and bid him go free. As we read in v.7, "the mind that is set on the flesh is hostile to God; it does not submit to God's law, indeed it cannot." The natural man is inevitably held in the grip of sin. He is like Bunyan's man in the iron cage who cries "I cannot get out: oh now, I cannot!" Paul himself had passed through that desolating experience. He was captive to the law of sin which was in his members: certainly as a Jewish enthusiast and probably even after his conversion before he tasted the fulness of the Spirit. If we are to regard 7:7–25 as autobiographical, as it seems we must, it would appear to relate to a period in Paul's spiritual development consequent upon his arrest on the Damascus road. As Dr. James Denney insisted, "no one could have written this passage but a Christian." He, however, felt that Paul was looking back on his pre-conversion days through regenerate eyes. It would seem more consistent with the evidence to consider this as part of his Christian conflict before the tension was resolved by the appropriation of the Spirit. Whether this took place during the three days in Damascus when he was without sight (Acts 9:9) or, as would seem to be more likely, during his sojourn in Arabia (Gal. 1:17), we are not told, and in the absence of a specific disclosure in Scripture we are wise to refrain from speculation. But that the emancipation occurred can hardly be open to doubt and in this verse Paul himself tells us that it was the work of the Spirit.

The second factor in Paul's spiritual rebirth and emancipation from law was *the liberator Spirit.* Paul recognized the operation of the Third Person of the Trinity in his rescue. The agent of his liberation was the Holy Ghost. "Where the Spirit of the Lord is, there is freedom" (II Cor. 3:17).

He is indeed "the Spirit of life." He has life and He conveys life. He is, as the Nicene Creed invites us to affirm, "the Lord and Giver of life." That is His characteristic function. He was the life-bringer at creation: "the Spirit of God was moving over the face of the waters" (Gen. 1:2). He is the life-bringer in regeneration: "Unless one is born of water and the Spirit, he cannot enter the kingdom of God" (John 3:5). He is the life-bringer in sanctification: "that according to the riches of his glory he may grant you to be strengthened with might through his Spirit in the inner man, and that Christ may dwell in your hearts through faith; that you, being rooted and grounded in love . . . may be filled with all the fulness of God." (Eph. 3:16,17,19). He is the life-bringer in resurrection: "If the Spirit of him who raised Jesus from the dead dwells in you, he who raised Christ Jesus from the dead will give life to your mortal bodies also through his Spirit which dwells in you" (Rom. 8:11). So here it is the Holy Spirit who applies the liberating law to the believer's soul. "He writes the law of God with living fire in our hearts," said Luther, "and consequently the law is not doctrine but life, not word but reality, not a sign but very fulness." This is the work of the liberator Spirit. He is the Spirit of life.

But all He does is "in Christ Jesus." The Spirit is the Spirit of Christ. He operates in and through the Son, God has no gifts for us out of Christ, not even the gift of the Spirit. It is the Spirit who brings life, but the life He brings is Christ. The Spirit is the vehicle, but it is "Christ who is our life" (Col. 3:4), just as the Spirit is the Sanctifier but Christ is the sanctification (I Cor. 1:30). "The Spirit is never regarded as the *content* of the quickened life," Fr. Lionel Thornton concludes after carefully examining the New Testament evidence. "The Spirit is the quickening cause; and the indwelling of Christ is the effect of the quickening."

The third factor in Paul's entry into the fulness of salvation and the Spirit's power was *the liberated life*. This is, so to speak, the end-product. When the new law governs and the Spirit enables, a life of liberty results. The twin tyrants of sin and death are deprived of their dictatorship. "*Has* set me free" – it is a realized liberation. As the aorist indicates, it is an event which has actually occurred. The believer is "saved from the guilt and strength of sin," to borrow a line of Charles Wesley. But we shall have more to say of this when we reach v.4.

III.   Paul proceeds to deal with THE SALVATION HE IS ENABLED TO ENGAGE (v.3). This has to do with the believer's equipment. It is significant that Dr. C. H. Dodd entitles this section from 1–4 "The Saving Act of God." This third verse sets out what God has already done in order that the Christian may be brought under the new law of the Spirit. In order to enter into the glorious liberty of the children of God, we do not have to manufacture any qualifications of our own. Righteousness by works has no more place here than in conversion. Salvation is altogether of God. And its benefits extend beyond the moment when the sinner trusts in Christ and leaves behind the old life of the flesh. The believer needs continually to lay hold on what has been wrought for him in Christ. If he is to be freed from the law of sin and death and submit to the promptings of the Spirit, he must draw daily upon that salvation which has been purchased for him at such a price. He engages its machinery, as it were, and gears it to the requirements of his ongoing discipleship.

This third verse speaks first about *the inability of the law*. It frankly faces what the law could not do. The law was not final. It was not the ultimate answer to sin. It set the standard of God's requirement, but it was helpless to enable man to meet it. The law was negative. It was made up mainly of prohibitions. "Thou shalt not" was its watchword. It could fling a barrier of warning across the broad way that led to destruction, but it could not turn men into the narrow way that alone leads to life eternal. It could prescribe appropriate rituals for the purification of defilement and restore external cleanness, but it was impotent to deal with inward sin. And as Dr. J. H. Jowett would insist, sin is heart trouble, not skin disease. The law could rebuke, admonish, condemn: it could not save. It could *point* out sin, but it could not *cast* out sin.

This, then, was the basic inability of the law. It was inadequate to produce what it required in the worshipper. It was full of demand: it made no offer. As Karl Barth puts it in his epoch-making exposition of Romans, "the law could not set human feet upon the rock of eternity and rid them of the sentence of death which had been pronounced over them." All this was involved in what the law could not do. "For no human being will be justified in his sight by works of the law since through the law comes knowledge of sin" (3:20). That conclusion was reached on the basis of this incapacity of the law to rescue from sin.

The reason for this impotence is indicated here in 8:3: it is because it is "weakened by the flesh," or, rather, "thwarted as it was by human frailty" (Weymouth). The law itself, of course, was not "weak through the flesh" (A.V.) except in the sense that it was what Hebrews 7:16 calls "a carnal commandment." It was man, to whom the law appealed, who was weakened by sin and thus prevented from obeying its behests. This fundamental incapacity of man deprived the law of its effectiveness. As the New English Bible expresses it, "our lower nature robbed it of all potency." "The voice of Sinai was powerless to save," declared Agar Beet, "because our flesh was too weak to throw off the bondage of sin."

This verse next speaks about *the capability of God*. What the law could not do, God did. What it could not effect, God effected. Paul gets so excited about this miracle of grace that he casts to the winds what he had learned about sentence structure and becomes breathlessly ungrammatical. His professor of rhetoric in the University of Tarsus would no doubt have disowned him, but he was under the higher tutelage of the Holy Spirit and was therefore permitted to break with human regulations. After "what the law, weakened by the flesh, could not do" at the beginning, we should expect a parallel clause something like "this God was able to do." Instead Paul is led to describe the very manner in which God was able to do this – "sending his own Son in the likeness of sinful flesh and for sin" – and the result which followed – "he condemned sin in the flesh" – without actually saying that He did it. But it is all quite clearly implied.

There is (a) the *means* by which God did what the law could not do. It was by the incarnation. God sent "his own Son" – there is tender emphasis here which recalls the parable of the wicked husbandmen in Mark 12:1–10. In v.32 of this same chapter in Romans we are reminded again that God did not spare even His own Son but gave Him up for us all. Christ came in the flesh. He shared our humanity. He wore the robe of human frame. "The Word became flesh and dwelt among us" (John 1:4).

But Paul has been talking about the law of sin and death which has its seat in the flesh – that is, in unredeemed humanity standing in the succession of Adam's sin. Our Lord Jesus Christ, of course, though He was made man, did not inherit original sin. By His unique birth He came into the world without sin, even as He lived a sinless life. It is true that He was made to be sin on our behalf, in the sense that He carried the curse of our transgressions, and this may be the import of the next phrase, "and for sin." But it was not actually sinful flesh that He entered.

It was the *likeness* of sinful flesh. Paul uses the same word in Philippians 2:7 when he says that our Lord took "the form of a servant, being born in the likeness of men." Professor Lenski's comment on 8:3 is pertinent as it draws attention to the precision of the Word at this point. " 'In likeness of flesh of sin' is one of those exact Scripture phrases which admit of no change. 'The likeness of flesh' would be Docetism, Christ would then be without real flesh; 'the flesh of sin' would be Ebionitism, Christ would then have had sinful flesh; but 'likeness of flesh of sin' is gospel doctrine, Christ assumed our flesh but not its sinfulness."

There is also (b) the *purpose* for which God sent His Son. It was simply "for sin." That could mean "for a sin offering" as it does in II Corinthians 5:21 (so R.V., N.E.B., R.S.V.mg.) This would chime in with the second of the three reasons for the Incarnation supplied in I John 4. At v.10 we read: "God . . . sent his Son to be the propitiation for our sins" (A.V.). The other equally significant reasons are to be found in verses 9 and 14.

But this interpolation is not strictly necessary, nor does the context demand such an interpretation. We may prefer to follow the Berkeley Version and render the phrase as "on account of sin." The whole matter of Christ's mission in respect of sin may well be included in such a compendious yet comprehensive formula. We recall a similar usage in Galatians 1:4 where Paul refers to our Lord Jesus Christ "who gave himself for our sins to deliver us from the present evil age" and in I Peter 3:18 where we are told that "Christ also died for sins once for all." In this case, however, as in the latter, the Greek preposition means "with reference to" and not as in Galatians 1:4 "on behalf of."

This, then, was the purpose God had in mind when He sent His Son. He came to deal with sin. Before there could be liberation, atonement had to be made. The new life in the Spirit is only possible on the ground of Christ's finished work at the Cross.

There is lastly (c) the *result* of what God did in the sending
of His Son. "He condemned sin in the flesh." He not only
pronounced His disapproval. He wrote its death-sentence.
The law could condemn by registering disapprobation.
God not only said how much He hated sin: He actually
did away with sin itself. He condemned it to death. He
punished it with all the severity it deserved. He executed
a capital sentence upon it.

This He did in the person of His beloved Son. The
meaning here is not that sin in the flesh was condemned
but that in the flesh sin was condemned, "He passed
judgment against sin within that very nature" (N.E.B.) –
i.e. in the likeness of which Christ had come. It was on the
site of man's previous defeat that the victory was gained.
Christ won our battle on our battlefield. As C. H. Dodd
helpfully explains it: "Christ entered the sphere which
Sin had claimed for its own (for we must needs personify
sin if we are to carry out the metaphor). Sin pressed his
claim against Christ, but lost his case. Christ was not
condemned: sin was. For Christ brought into the sphere
of the flesh the unimpaired power of the Spirit. And hence
it follows that those also who are 'in Christ' are no longer
condemned." Verse 3 is thus linked with verse 1.

IV.   But it is also linked with verse 4 as we shall now
see. Paul finally points to THE CONSUMMATION HE IS ENABLED
TO EMBODY (v.4). This has to do with the believer's exemplification. Not only does the Christian escape condemnation. He typifies in his own life and conduct the positive
objective of righteousness. He expresses in his daily walk
that holiness which is the goal God has in view for man
in Christ. Exonerated from sin, emancipated from law,
equipped by grace, he becomes a breathing embodiment
of God's purpose. "For this is the will of God, your sanctification" (I Thess. 4:4). The salvation wrought by the
sacrifice of Christ was not engineered simply as an exhibition
of God's power. It was intended to lead to a blessed end.
That end is holiness. As Paul had told the Galatians,

"If we live by the Spirit, let us also walk by the Spirit" (Gal. 5:25).

The righteousness of the law is not discarded but brought to fruition. All that God did in His Son for our redemption was "in order that the just requirement of the law might be fulfilled in us, who walk not according to the flesh but according to the Spirit" (v.4). The demands of the law are met when the righteousness of Christ is imparted to the believer by the Spirit, as well as imputed by the Father. The latter is the essence of justification. The former is the essence of sanctification. And so here in this verse, as Professor Kingsley Barrett reminds us, "the thought is not so much that what the law requires is righteous, as that what the law requires is righteousness." Righteousness *by* the law is an impossibility, as Paul has shown in verse 3. Righteousness *of* the law, that is the righteousness which the law demands but can never provide, is gloriously possible when the Spirit applies to our hearts the full benefits of Christ's atoning death. Our Lord is Himself possessed of that perfect righteousness and it is unique to Him. He alone has attained to God's moral standard and no one else ever will apart from Him. But He gained the goal not merely as a decoration: He won the prize so that He might share it with us. His righteousness is offered to believers through the Spirit. It becomes a rich reality in experience. That is the whole aim and intention of what Paul is here expounding. The just requirement of the law is to be fulfilled in us.

Underline that "*in us*." That is the place of exemplification. Not in heavenly angels: in *us*. Not in haloed saints: in *us*. Not in spiritual specialists: in *us*. That is the objective of redemption. Christ died not only that we might be forgiven: He died to make us good. "You must therefore be all goodness," He said, "just as your heavenly Father is all good" (Matt. 5:48 N.E.B.) – and He shed His precious blood to open up the way. His incarnation, atonement, resurrection, ascension and intercession all have this single aim. And everything God works within us: awakening, repentance, faith, justification, regeneration, sanctification – all these Divine acts of mercy have only one goal – that the righteousness of the law might be fulfilled in us. "But now that you have been set free from sin," Paul has already written to the Romans, "and have become slaves of God, the return you get is sanctification and its end, eternal life" (6:22).

Sanctification by the Spirit is classified by Beet as the fifth and last fundamental doctrine of this epistle. The new life Christ came to impart is implanted by the Holy Spirit. It is not something we have to work *up* in ourselves: it is something that is worked *down* by God. Sanctification is no more of works than is justification. Holiness, like salvation, is a gift of God received in faith.

> *Holiness by faith in Jesus,*
> *Not by effort of thine own,*
> *Sin's dominion crushed and broken*
> *By the power of grace alone.*
> *God's own holiness within thee,*
> *His own beauty on thy brow:*
> *This shall be thy pilgrim brightness,*
> *This thy blessed portion now.*

We close this study with some encouraging words from Dr. Beet. "When God bids us reckon ourselves dead to sin, and henceforth living only for Him, we remember our moral weakness, and say, How can these things be? But when we learn that henceforth the Spirit of God will dwell within us in order that by His power He may protect us from all sin, and by His holiness direct towards God our every purpose and effort – when we learn this, our doubt gives place to confident expectation and adoring gratitude. For we are sure that the Spirit is able to accomplish even in us, God's purpose of holiness."

CHAPTER THREE

THE MIND OF THE SPIRIT

WHEN WE MOVE ON, AS WE NOW DO, to the fifth verse of Romans Eight, the main theme from Chapter Five onwards is resumed, and Paul's exposition takes a notable step forward. In order to appreciate this development of thought, we shall have to look back at that highly significant verse in the Fifth Chapter which speaks about the power and motive of the new and sanctified life (v.5). Weigh it again: "God's love has been poured out in our hearts through the Holy Spirit Who has been given to us" (Amplified New Testament). In a very real sense that is the germ statement from which the apostle's entire argument in this section unfolds. But it is only taken up again in the Eighth Chapter. The Spirit here returns to prominence. That is why we can rightly describe it as the Pentecost of Romans.

Already in verses 1–4, as we have seen, the unlimited and indeed illimitable possibilities of life by the Spirit have been suggested. Now from v.5 on, down to v.8, Paul expands his own testimony by drawing a sharp contrast between life in the Spirit and its unsatisfactory opposite, namely life in the flesh. This "great either-or," as it has been called, has been hinted at in the opening paragraph of this Chapter (see v.1 in A.V. and v.4). In a previous letter, to the Galatians, Paul had handled the same subject: "But, I say, walk by the Spirit, and do not gratify the desires of the flesh. For the desires of the flesh are against the Spirit, and the desires of the Spirit are against the flesh; for these are opposed to each other, to prevent you from doing what you would. But if you

are led by the Spirit you are not under the law" (Gal.
5:16–18). Then follow the successive catalogues: the works
of the flesh and the fruit of the Spirit (vv.19–23). It is
quite obvious that in Galatians Paul had precisely the
same situation in mind as here in Romans. "What you
will to do you cannot do" (Gal. 5:17 N.E.B.) is a summary
of Romans 7:7–25. Romans Eight shows the solution as
lying in the direction of the Spirit rather than of the
law.

The consequence of this Spirit-filled and Spirit-guided
life is that the tensions of Chapter Seven are resolved.
The mortal combat between flesh and spirit is settled,
because the flesh has been crucified with Christ. The
believer enjoys the peaceful fruits of victory. Not that he
is immune from attack. On the contrary, Satan is selective
in his targets and directs his fiercest offensive against the
Christian. "The devil tempteth not unbelievers and sinners,"
noted Thomas á Kempis, "whom he hath already secure
possession of, but faithful and religious devout persons he
in various ways tempteth and disquieteth." But he is no
longer permitted to gain the upper hand. That was what
John Wesley discovered after his conversion. Immediately
following that transforming encounter in Aldersgate
Street, he added in his *Journal:* "After my return home,
I was much buffetted with temptations; but cried out,
and they fled away. They returned again and again.
I as often lifted up my eyes and He 'sent me help from
His holy place.' And herein I found the difference between
this and my former state chiefly consisted. I was striving,
yea, fighting with all my might under the law, as well
as under grace. But then I was sometimes, if not often,
conquered; now I was always conqueror." Indeed, it
would be a poor sort of Gospel which kept us in lifelong
captivity to sin. "What would be the use of the new birth
or redemption at all," enquired Johannes Weiss with
some justifiable heat, "if it could not end that miserable
stress and slavery?" In Chapter Six Paul has supplied
us with the greatest negative in Scripture – v.14 "For sin

shall *not* have dominion over you" (A.V.) Now he proceeds
to expand that claim in positive terms.

But before we go any further we must endeavour to
clarify and crystallize Scripture teaching on sanctification
as it relates to the conflict with sin. Let us immediately
endorse some most instructive words of Octavius Winslow
in his choice and classic study, *The Work of the Spirit*.
"The notion, so fondly cherished by some, of perfect
sinlessness here, is as fatal to true sanctification as it is
contrary to God's Word. They know but little of their
own heart, who do not know, that sin (to borrow the
language of John Owen), 'not only still abides in us,
but is still acting, still labouring to bring forth the deeds
of the flesh.' They know little who do not know that in
their 'flesh there dwelleth no good thing,' that 'that which
is born of the flesh is flesh,' and will retain its fleshly
nature and propensities to the very last. Let us not exult
'as though we had already attained, or were already perfect:' let us not be 'ignorant of Satan's devices,' one of
which is to build us up in the belief that, in the present
life, a man may cease from the work of mortification.
The Lord keep the reader from cherishing so erroneous
an idea. The work of sanctification is the work of a man's
life. 'When sin lets us alone (as has been remarked) we
may let sin alone.' But when is the day, indeed, when is
the hour, that sin does not strive for the mastery, and in
which the believer can say that he has completely slain
his enemy? He may, 'through the Spirit, mortify the deeds
of the body,' and if he does, 'he shall live;' but as the heart
is the natural and luxurious soil of every noxious weed of
sin, and as another springs up as soon as one is cut down,
indeed as the *same root* appears again above the surface
with new life and vigour, it requires a ceaseless care and
vigilance, a perpetual mortification of sin in the body,
until we throw off this cumbrous clay and go where sin
is known no more."

Whenever we dwell upon this vital theme of holiness,
such considerations should always loom large in the fore-

ground of our minds. But this is not to deprive the believer of the genuine victory he may enjoy even in this mortal life. Scripture assures that, when armed with the accoutrement of God's provision, the Christian will "be *able* to stand against the wiles of the devil" (Eph. 6:11), "*able* to withstand in the evil day" (v.13), and "*can* quench all the flaming darts of the evil one" (v.16). So, with the preceding proviso fully in view, we can nevertheless affirm from God's Word that for the believer there is no inevitability of moral failure. The Christian need not sin. God has devised an escape route from temptation. Satan was defeated at the Cross and so, in Christ, can be defeated still. It is not claimed that the Christian *cannot* sin, nor is it observed empirically that he *does* not sin, for this would be to fly in the face of fact. But as long as he walks in the Spirit and not in the flesh, he *will* not sin. If, however, he fails so to walk, he may very easily fall also. "What the apostle here declares," wrote Evan Hopkins, one of the founders of the Keswick Convention, referring to the parallel passage from Galatians, "is that 'walking in the Holy Ghost' is the means of living in continual triumph over, or in a state of deliverance from, 'the lust of the flesh'."

Some characteristically shrewd and considered words of Oswald Chambers – how often we turn profitably to him for illumination! – will serve to wind up this excursus. This is from his *Philosophy of Sin*. "The inclination to sin, thank God, is removed, but never the possibility. If the power to disobey were removed, our obedience would be of no value, for we should cease to be morally responsible. It is gloriously possible not to sin, but never impossible to sin, because we are moral agents. Morality must be militant in this order of things, but we can be 'more than conquerors' every time."

Now let us look a little more closely at this contrast between the flesh-life and the Spirit-life contained in Romans 8:5–8. Verses 1 and 4 have referred to the Christian's walk. Verse 5 goes deeper and has to do with the

Christian's essential being. This is literally an ontological statement, for the Greek participle *ontes* from which that philosophical term is derived appears here in the text. The Authorized Version is strictly accurate when it reads: "For they that *are* after the flesh . . . they that *are* after the Spirit" (although the participle is not actually repeated but implied in the second part of the clause). We shall discover that there is a sequence of contrasts in this section, with a different one in each verse.

I. First we meet THE CONTRAST OF AMBITION in v.5. Professor Kingsley Barrett says that this verse is a definition. It tells us exactly in what the flesh-life and the Spirit-life consist. It is a question of mind or objective. The verb used here really means to pursue or set the heart on. It is to have a concern so constantly in mind that it becomes almost an obsession. It represents the preoccupation or absorption of the total personality, for it involves the emotions and will as well as the reason. What Paul is talking about here is the dominant interest of a man's life, the bent of his desire, the goal of all his activities. So we may quite legitimately employ the concept of ambition, for that is the focus of his aim.

The apostle contrasts those whose ambition in life is solely concerned with the flesh and those whose ambition in life is solely concerned with the Spirit. We must find out what is meant by the flesh-life and the Spirit-life.

The Greek for flesh is *sarx* and it occurs no less than ninety-one times in the Pauline letters. It does not always represent precisely the same thing: if it did, exegesis would be much simpler. According to Dr. Wheeler Robinson, its usages may be classified under five variations of significance. (1) Sometimes it means physical structure, anatomical tissue and tegument, as when we speak of flesh and blood (Rom. 2:28 – our references will be confined to this epistle). (2) Sometimes it means kinship, or human relations (Rom. 1:3; 4:1; 9:3,5,8; 11:14). (3) Sometimes it means the sphere or condition of our present existence (not in Rom., but *cf*. Gal. 2:20). (4) Sometimes it means the weakness of our nature, either bodily or mental (Rom. 6:19). (5) Sometimes it signifies an ethical experience, and it is with this most frequent and important connotation that we are now concerned.

In this usage of *sarx* it is implied that there is a general relationship between the flesh and sin and that somehow the flesh is active in the production of evil. Now it is with this fifth and commonest meaning that flesh is mentioned here in Romans Eight. Paul is not contrasting the life *in* the Spirit with the life *in* the flesh: he is contrasting the life *of* the Spirit with the life *of* the flesh, or *according to* the flesh. Our Lord Jesus Christ Himself lived *in* the flesh: but He did not live *by* the flesh.

What, then, is flesh in this sense? Although Dr. Robinson described it as an ethical experience, it really goes beyond that. It has ethical consequences, of course, but perhaps nowadays we should call it an existential experience – that is to say, having to do with the essential meaning of life. Involved in this distinction between flesh and spirit is the fundamental decision which no man can evade. Flesh, then, is the life of man apart from the touch of God. It is human nature on its material level, divorced from any contact with the spiritual. Calvin described it as whatever is outside Christ. And, since apart from Him we can do nothing, flesh is humanity in its weakness and sinfulness and its desperate need of help. Melanchthon declared that it was "the entire nature of man without the Holy Spirit." "What, indeed, does flesh mean," asks Karl Barth, "but the complete inadequacy of the creature when he stands before the Creator?" In a word, flesh is man adrift from God.

How relevant all this now turns out to be in relation to our contemporary world! Flesh is the life of the average man today, lived as it is outside the Divine context. It is the typical existence of *homo sapiens* in the sixties, conditioned by the assumptions of scientific materialism. Its ambition is set solely upon the affairs of this life. It lacks any super-

natural content. Those who "mind the things of the flesh,"
said Wesley, are those who "have their thoughts and
affections fixed on such things as gratify corrupt nature:
namely, on things visible and temporal; on things of the
earth, on pleasure (of sense or imagination), praise, or
riches." That might be a picture of space-age man!

In contrast to this purely material preoccupation,
the Christian believer is to set his mind on the things of
the Spirit. He really lives in another world. His motives
and objectives are altogether different. He sits lightly
to all things temporal. He is supremely concerned with
the spiritual. The things that interest the worldly man
will not interest him. His sights are trained on a higher
target. He sets his mind "on things that are above, not
on things that are on earth" (Col. 3:2). It is this elevation
of ambition which underlies the life of holiness.

II. Next we have THE CONTRAST OF CONDITION in v.6.
The absolute incompatibility between these two modes of
living is underscored by the "for" at the beginning of this
sixth verse in the Authorized Version. The ambitions
of the flesh arise from the condition of the flesh, just as the
ambitions of the spirit arise from the condition of the
spirit. Paul here depicts this difference in state or condition
as one between death and life. No contrast could be greater.

The subject of the sentence is "the mind of the flesh."
It is a substantive, as the New English Bible brings out,
and not a verbal form as the Authorized Version would
imply. As A. T. Robertson explains, moreover, it is not
the mind that does the minding, nor the action of minding
(for there are other words for these) but the result of the
action – what is minded, or the attitude produced. This
outlook spells death. And Paul means a present death.
He is not simply asserting, as in Chapter Five, that physical
death is the entail of sin. He intends us to understand that
the flesh brings death now, as well as at the end. "For the
wages of sin *is* death" (Rom. 6:23): not "will be death"
but "is." And in the Greek there is not even a verb in

that verse. No word at all intervenes between sin and death, so closely are they interrelated. "The wages of sin – death!" So here in 8:6 no verb intrudes: as can be inferred from the italics in the Authorized Version, "is" does not reflect anything in the original. Paul simply says, "The mind of the flesh – death!" And it is death *now*: "death that comprises all the miseries arising from sin, both here and hereafter" (Amplified New Testament).

So then, those who make the flesh their ambition are even at this present moment entombed in death. They are not really alive at all. They are simply going through the motions. How different is the viewpoint of God's Word from the viewpoint of the world! Those who are absorbed in the flesh imagine that they have found life. They are seeing life, they think. They are making the most of life: they are sampling the spice of life. But God pronounces them dead: "dead through . . . trespasses and sins" (Eph. 2:1). They are sowing the seeds of final destruction. "She who is self-indulgent," Paul tells Timothy. "is dead even while she lives" (I Tim. 5:6).

By contrast, according to this sixth verse of Romans Eight, the mind of the Spirit is life. Once again the verb is absent: "the mind of the Spirit – life!" So intimately are life and the Spirit associated that they cannot even be separated by the tiniest word. They go absolutely together, for He is the Spirit of life (Rom. 8:2). Dean Alford called this "the suppressed premiss" of verse six.

We must take note of the life that is alluded to here. Another dip into Greek vocabulary will help us. It was Bishop Westcott who declared that it is possible to bury one's head in a lexicon and rise in the presence of God. Two terms for life are found in the New Testament. Each can be recognized from words in common English use. The first is *bios*. In Scripture that stands for physical life, either in animals or men. It is "biological" life. The narrative of one such human life is a "biography." But there is another word which the New Testament employs to denote the higher life of the Spirit. It is *zōe*. Now the strange thing is that in classical Greek *zōe* is used as inferior to *bios*. *Bios* is life as lived in extent – the duration of days: whereas *zōe* is the life by which we live, the principle of life. The Bible reverses the order and lifts *zōe* to the pinnacle of supremacy. The reason is not far to seek. For the believer, the principle of life is something more than breath. It is the Spirit Himself. He is the breath of our new life in Christ, and so *zōe* is raised to another plane and signifies the life of God in the regenerate soul of man.

That is the word used here by Paul. It indicates that spiritual, everlasting life is the contrast to the death of sin (cf. Rom. 6:23). *Zōe* is the very life of God Himself communicated by the Spirit. It is the life that has not been touched by sin and death. As Archbishop Trench has pointed out in his celebrated study of New Testament synonyms, it is essentially the life of holiness. In its distinctively Christian usage, *zōe* assumes the profoundest moral significance and becomes the fittest expression for the very highest blessedness. "Of that whereof I predicate absolute *zōe*, I predicate absolute holiness of the same. Christ affirming of Himself, *egō eimi hē zōe* (I am the life, John 14:6 cf. I John 1:2), implicitly affirmed of Himself that He was absolutely holy; and in the creature, in like manner, that only *lives*, or triumphs over death, death at once physical and spiritual, which has first triumphed over sin. No wonder, then, that Scripture should know no higher word than *zōe* to set forth the blessedness of God, and the blessedness of the creature in communion with God."

III. Now we pass to THE CONTRAST OF RELATION in v.7. Here we are given the reason why the flesh-mind is death and the Spirit-mind is life. "For:" that introduces an explanation (A.V. has "because"). The relation of the carnal mind to God is one of hostility. It is enmity against Him. This is in contrast to the relation of the spiritual mind to God. That, as we see from the last word in v.6 (which belongs logically to v.7), is one of peace. War and peace, then, is the distinction here.

The flesh is not only dead in itself: it is actively opposed to God. Matthew Henry thought that this was a worse state than the first. "The former speaks the carnal sinner a *dead* man, which is bad; but this speaks him a *devil* of a man."

This rebellion against God expresses itself in disobedience to His holy law. "It does not *submit* to God's law." The verb is a military one. It describes soldiers lined up on parade, or in battle array, united under the authority of their commander. General Gordon used to stand to attention before God at the beginning of each new day. He recognized the Divine sovereignty. That is just what the natural man refuses to do. He will have no-one telling him what to do, not even God. This is an inevitable consequence of the fleshly outlook. It develops a warped view of God. It cannot see Him as a loving Father. It only envisages a stern taskmaster from whom it recoils in arrogant defiance. "If any one loves the world," says John, "love for the Father is not in him" (I John 2:15). That is his tragedy. It is simply not in him to love God, or to recognize God's claim, or submit to His wise and beneficent law.

The determinism of sin lies at the root of this inability. It is in recognition of such a spiritual atrophy that Paul adds here: "indeed it cannot." The flesh-minded life is inherently unable to fulfil the Divine requirement. Selfishness cannot submit to God. Sin cannot obey. It would be a contradiction in terms if it could, for the Bible says that sin is lawlessness. It is the ultimate anarchy. If it were able to comply with God's demand, it would not be sin.

This appears to some as a hard saying. It even seems to smack of an unfashionable predestinarianism. It is nevertheless the uniform doctrine of God's Word. The man who lives according to the flesh not only refuses to acknowledge the Divine authority: he can do no other. He is enslaved by stern moral and spiritual necessity. Just as God cannot deny Himself and therefore cannot do other than good, so the natural man, so to speak, cannot deny himself either, and therefore cannot do other than evil. "*Can the*

Ethiopian change his skin, or the leopard his spots? Then also you can do good who are accustomed to do evil" (Jer. 13:23).

This was the clear teaching of our Lord, both in its positive and negative aspects. He said that the ungodly can do nothing other than be ungodly and that they cannot of themselves enter into His kingdom. "Are grapes gathered from thorns, or figs from thistles? So, every sound tree bears good fruit, but the bad tree bears evil fruit. A sound tree *cannot* bear evil fruit, nor *can* a bad tree bear good fruit." (Matt. 7:16–18). "Unless one is born anew, he *cannot* see the kingdom of God" (John 3:3). "Unless one is born of water and the Spirit, he *cannot* enter the kingdom of God" (John 3:5). "No one *can* come to me unless the Father who sent me draws him" (John 6:44). "No one *can* come to me unless it is granted him by the Father" (John 6:65). "You *cannot* bear to hear my word" (John 8:43). The Spirit of truth is He "whom the world *cannot* receive, because it neither sees Him nor knows him" (John 14:17).

The same insistence recurs elsewhere in the New Testament. "The unspiritual man does not receive the gifts of the Spirit of God, for they are folly to him, and he is *not able* to understand them, because they are spiritually discerned" (I Cor. 2:14). That is the consistent and unequivocal testimony of God's Word. Man under the flesh is at enmity with his Maker. He will not obey: indeed he cannot. That is his relation to God: one of hostile resistance.

The believer, on the other hand, is no longer at war against God. He has capitulated to the Divine conqueror. He has been reconciled by the blood of Christ. His relation to the Father is one of perfect peace, and this produces peace in his own mind and soul, as the fruit of the Spirit.

This is what our modern world is seeking, with its craze for tranquillizing drugs and psychiatric treatment. It has lost its peace. It hopes to find it again in the chemist's shop or the psycho-analyst's consulting room. But that is a vain endeavour. Peace can be found only in God and in conformity to His will. It is a by-product of the Spirit-mind. Dr. C. H. Dodd seeks to draw out the profound psychological implications of Paul's affirmation here when he writes that such peace is "the condition of inward harmony when all elements of the personality are organized about a single centre, and division and conflict are at an end." That is the cherished goal of man's frantic striving in this age. He can orbit the earth and soon he may land on the moon, but the target of peace eludes him. It is attainable only in God. "Thou dost keep him in perfect peace, whose mind is stayed on thee, because he trusts in thee" (Isa. 26:3).

In the preface to his best-known book, Billy Graham has written: "I am convinced that there is a great hunger of mind and thirst of soul on the part of the average man for peace with God." Unless that hunger and thirst is satisfied in Christ, it will continue to undermine man's vitality. Unless the Church takes Christ to the people who need Him so much, they will still be frustrated. Those who know must reach those who don't. Evangelism, according to Daniel Niles, is "one poor beggar telling another poor beggar where to get bread." God's peace is not to be monopolized but shared.

IV. Last of all we come to THE CONTRAST OF PROBATION in verse 8. The final distinction between the flesh-life and the Spirit-life is now drawn. It is an addition to what has preceded, not only a logical consequence of it, as the "so then" of the Authorized Version would suggest. "Furthermore," the apostle continues, "those who are in the flesh cannot please God." Again, there is the note of moral necessity. Paul is not only declaring that in point of fact those who lead the life of the flesh do not succeed in satisfying God: he goes further and claims that they are actually incapable of doing so.

This is a contrast of probation. These two types of character are put to the test. They are submitted to

Divine inspection. God makes trial of them. He proves them in order to discover whether they reach the standard He requires. He can be pleased only with what is good and righteous. He takes no delight in sin. As the test is made, the distinction appears. It marks off those who serve the flesh from those who serve the Spirit. The former are disapproved by God: only the latter are pleasing in His sight. The contrast is quite clear-cut. There is no convenient merging of margins. Those who live to please themselves cannot possibly please God. Our Lord told us no less: "No one can serve two masters; for either he will hate the one and love the other, or he will be devoted to the one and despise the other. You cannot serve God and mammon" (Matt. 6:24).

The Bible has much to say about the need to please God. As Christians, we are not to please ourselves (Rom. 15:1). We are to please our neighbour for his good, to edify him (Rom. 15:2). Even Christ did not please Himself (Rom. 15:3). But most of all we are to please God, as the Saviour did and does (John 8:29). We are "to lead a life worthy of the Lord, fully pleasing to him" (Col. 1:10). We are to "keep his commandments and do what pleases him" (I John 3:22). It is Paul's claim with respect to the Thessalonians that they learned from him and his fellow evangelists how they "ought to live and to please God" (I Thess. 4:1). It is the great concluding prayer of Hebrews that the God of peace would equip them with everything good that they might do His will, working in them that which is pleasing in His sight (Heb. 13:21).

Those who persist in fleshly pursuits, who tread the world's path and refuse to be led of the Spirit, obviously cannot prove pleasing to God. "Without faith it is impossible to please him" (Heb. 11:6). Even when such a man plays at being religious – for that is the best he can do – he still cannot deceive God. "The sacrifice of the wicked is an abomination to the Lord" (Prov. 15:8). It is not the gift that comes under scrutiny, but the giver; not the prayer, but the pray-er; not the worship, but the worshipper. We are told in Genesis 4:4 that "the Lord had regard for Abel and his offering" and similarly in the following verse that "for Cain and his offering he had no regard." The person comes first, and unless God is pleased with us, He cannot be placated by our offerings. However he may try, the flesh-directed man can by no means satisfy God.

Only the Spirit-directed man can do that. It is not that he possesses any merits of his own, but he has submitted himself to God. He trusts in Christ: he relies on the Spirit. The Father is always well-pleased with His Son, and when He looks on us as found in Him, He is well-pleased with us too. That is our plea and our hope, and it will not fail. Only in Christ and by the Spirit can we please God.

This, then, is the mind of the Spirit, in contrast to the mind of the flesh. To be precise, what is set over against the carnal life is the spiritual. The flesh is not directly opposed to the Spirit, for that would be to measure the altogether human by the altogether Divine. It is contrasted with the spirit – the human *pneuma*, which in the regenerate believer is united with the Divine and combines to provide the twofold testimony referred to in verse 16 of this chapter. This spiritual mind is a totally other outlook. It has a different ambition or objective in view. It is in a different state or condition. It stands in a different relation to God. And it receives a different verdict from Him when put to the proof. It seeks only to gain His smile and that is its all-sufficient reward.

It is said that when one of Verdi's earliest and shoddiest operas was produced in Florence, the enthusiastic but undiscriminating audience went into quite unwarranted raptures and cheered the composer to the echo. But Verdi paid little heed. He raised his eyes to where the great genius Rossini sat in stony silence. That was the opinion which mattered most. Unless he satisfied the maestro, the plaudits of the crowd meant nothing. May we learn to scorn the empty praise of men if only we may win the approval of heaven.

CHAPTER FOUR

THE POWER OF THE SPIRIT

As WE PASS FROM VERSE 8 TO VERSE 9 of this Pentecostal Eighth Chapter of Romans, we are conscious of a shifted emphasis. The section 5–8 has dealt with the mind of the Spirit, but, as we have seen, it did so by way of contrast. The life which reflects the outlook of the Spirit is delineated in a negative fashion by setting it over against its opposite, namely, the life of the flesh. The conclusion of the matter is reached in verse 8 when Paul sums up the case by saying that "those who are in the flesh cannot please God."

Now he proceeds on the positives. He goes on to describe the way of the Spirit in more direct terms. He shows what it is, not simply by contrasting it with the flesh-life, but by affirming what it is in itself. As Professor Barrett comments here: "Paul is in process of developing a new definition of the Christian life." The essence of the Spirit's effect on the believing soul can be expressed in a single word – power. Power is a much-used term today. We speak of power-play in sport and of power-politics in the realm of international affairs. We are aware of the power of wealth and the power of publicity. But in this scientific age the power of which we are most conscious is that of natural energy, especially that which is concentrated in the atom. We live in a power-conditioned world.

That is why the Christian message concerning spiritual power ought not to fall on altogether deaf ears. It is geared to our times. It should ring a responsive bell in people's minds. At least they should understand something of what we are talking about. An age that has witnessed the disclosure and application of nuclear energy should be better able to appreciate the miracle of Pentecost. For what happened at the first Whitsuntide constituted a discovery in the spiritual realm comparable to the splitting of the atom in the scientific field.

The Holy Spirit is inseparably associated with power. That is the constant witness of Scripture. He is essentially the Spirit of power. This, of course, is because He is the Lord and giver of life. We might say that His is a ministry of life and power. Consider some of the relevant passages in the New Testament. When Mary is told by the angel that she is to be the mother of Jesus, Gabriel adds: "The Holy Spirit will come upon you, and the *power* of the Most High will overshadow you" (Luke 1:35). At His temptation we read that our Lord was "led by the Spirit for forty days in the wilderness" (Luke 4:1) and that afterwards He "returned in the *power* of the Spirit into Galilee" (Luke 4:14). It was because of His endowment by the Spirit, Who descended upon Him in the visible form of a dove at His Baptism, that our Lord was enabled to perform His many miracles, and which, in particular, accounts for His ability to cast out evil spirits (Luke 5:17). The spectators of such exorcisms were "all amazed and said to one another, 'What is this word? For with authority and *power* he commands the unclean spirits, and they come out' " (Luke 4:36).

Our Lord firmly promised that the power He Himself possessed through the Holy Spirit would be transmitted to His disciples. Already this had been hinted at earlier in His ministry. When the seventy returned from their mission, rejoicing that even the demons were subject to them in the name of Jesus, He looked forward to the ultimate victory. "I saw Satan fall like lightning from heaven. Behold, I have given you authority to tread upon serpents and scorpions, and over all the *power* of the enemy; and nothing shall hurt you" (Luke 10:18,19). But it was only at His Ascension that the promise was fully made. "And behold, I send the promise of my Father upon you;

but stay in the city, until you are clothed with *power* from on high" (Luke 24:49). That is confirmed in Acts 1:8 – "But you shall receive *power* when the Holy Spirit has come upon you." And when indeed, as Christ had foretold, the apostles continued His own wonderful works of healing, the question was inevitably raised, "By what *power* or by what name did you do this?" (Acts 4:7). Peter made it plain that it was not by their own power or piety (Acts 3:12), but by the power of the Holy Spirit and in the name of Jesus. We are told in Acts 6:5 that Stephen was "a man full of faith and of the Holy Spirit:" in almost the next breath, and following the same grammatical construction, we learn that he was "full of grace and *power*" (v.8) – a clear equation of the Spirit with power. And in his sermon prior to the Gentile Pentecost at Caesarea, Peter preached about Jesus of Nazareth whom God had anointed "with the Holy Spirit and with *power*" (Acts 10:38). It is noticeable, incidentally, that Luke lives up to his title as the evangelist of the Spirit, for all the foregoing references are from his writings.

But Luke, of course, does not stand in isolation in this testimony. In his letters Paul frequently makes the same association. In Romans 15:13 he prays: "May the God of hope fill you with all joy and peace in believing, so that by the *power* of the Holy Spirit you may abound in hope." In v.19 he refers to the mighty signs and wonders which were performed through him "by the *power* of the Holy Spirit." In I Corinthians 2:4 he says that his preaching was "not in plausible words of wisdom, but in demonstration of the Spirit and *power*." In Ephesians 3:7 he speaks about the grace-gift of the Spirit bestowed upon him "by the working of his *power*." And in II Timothy 1:7 he says: "God did not give us a spirit of timidity but a spirit of *power* and love and self-control." That last passage may well refer to our spirit, as the decapitalization of the Revised Standard Version indicates: but it is nevertheless our spirit as touched and transformed by the Spirit of God. It is, then, the concerted testimony of the

New Testament Scriptures that the Holy Spirit is the source of power. And this, of course, is what the Old Testament has also prepared us for. "But as for me," cries Micah, "I am filled with *power*, with the Spirit of the Lord" (Micah 3:8).

In this section of Romans Eight we are led to see how, step by step, the Holy Spirit becomes the source of power in the believer's life. For it is Christians who are being addressed here. "You" is emphatic by position in verse 9. "But you," Paul tells the Roman converts, –"you whose faith is proclaimed in all the world" (Rom. 1:8) – "are not in the flesh, you are in the Spirit." That is at once a reference back to the contrast between flesh and spirit contained in the previous passage (5–8) and an introduction of the next theme. For the first thing we learn in the portion before us now (9–12) is that the Spirit of power is

I. THE INDWELLING SPIRIT (v.9a). Paul has said already that the Roman believers are "in the Spirit." Now he assumes that, as this is indeed so, the Spirit must be in them. Just as elsewhere in his epistles the apostle uses "in Christ" and "Christ in you" almost as interchangeable terms, since they represent two aspects of the same spiritual experience, so here "you in the Spirit" and "the Spirit in you" are also intimately related. This, of course, is because He is the Spirit of Christ, as we see at the end of this ninth verse. C. H. Dodd explains that the Greek word for Spirit, when used in an ordinary context, denotes a kind of rarefied atmosphere: you can live in an atmosphere, and at the same time breathe it in. The Christian at once dwells in the Spirit's environment and yet is indwelt by the Spirit, Who is his inspiration (literally, something breathed in).

This is the first secret of the Spirit's power. As Samuel Chadwick put it: "Our Lord promised that the indwelling presence of the Spirit of God should be in men the all-prevailing source of power." The verb employed here for "dwell" is a very simple one. It is derived from the

Greek for a house. It means to live as in a home (I Cor. 7:12,13). The Spirit of God thus takes up His abode with us. He resides within. He moves in as an occupant, just as a man and wife might enter a new house. He makes our hearts His home. He is the Guest Divine: or, more appropriately, the Host who presides over all.

One of the great but forgotten preachers of a former generation, T. G. Selby – the friend and contemporary of Dr. W. L. Watkinson – had a memorable sermon on "The Three Indwellings." His text was taken from I John 4:16 – "He who abides in love abides in God, and God abides in him" – which he called "the primal gravitational law of the spiritual universe." He elaborated most tellingly on the interabiding of God and man in each other. This reciprocal relationship he took to be definitive in Christian experience. That is the theme of this ninth verse in Romans Eight, viewed from the angle of the Spirit. Three indwellings are mentioned here also, but the first is the fatal indwelling of the unregenerate in the flesh. Its counterpart is the equally lethal indwelling of sin in the unemancipated heart (Rom. 7:17,20). But "in the Spirit" and "the Spirit of God . . . . in you" is equivalent to John's "in God, and God . . . . in him." And John himself in an earlier verse (I John 4:13) has linked it with the work of the Spirit. "By this we know that we abide in him, because he has given us of his own Spirit."

Paul tells Timothy that God "dwells in unapproachable light" (I Tim. 6:16). What an astonishing thing it is that the selfsame word can be used of the Holy Spirit indwelling the believer! God is at home in the light, for God is light. The Holy Spirit is at home in the cleansed heart, for that is where God willed that He should reside. The wonder of it is perhaps nowhere better expressed than in Frederick Lucian Hosmer's hymn:

> *Go not, my soul in search of Him,*
> *Thou wilt not find Him there,*
> *Or in the depths of shadow dim,*
> *Or heights of upper air.*

For not in far-off realms of space
The Spirit hath His throne;
In every heart He findeth place
And waiteth to be known.

O gift of gifts! O grace of grace,
That God should condescend
To make thy heart His dwelling place
And be thy daily Friend!

"Do you not know that you are God's temple," Paul asks in I Corinthians 3:16, "and that God's Spirit dwells in you?" And again, in I Corinthians 6:19 – "Do you not know that your body is a temple of the Holy Spirit within you, which you have from God?" The apostle, of course, is addressing only believers, and we have to interpret "every heart" in the hymn just quoted by the light of such a restriction.

"What this expression 'dwell in you' imports," wrote Robert Haldane, "is that being united to Jesus Christ, and regenerated, the Holy Spirit dwells in His people not as inactive, but operates in them continually, and leads and governs them. In the indwelling, then, of the Holy Spirit, is included His gracious and continuing presence and His operations in the soul. The effects of these are illumination, sanctification, supplication and consolation." And here is what one of the early Christian fathers said concerning the Holy Spirit: "He is the author of regeneration, the pledge of the promised inheritance, and, as it were, the handwriting of eternal salvation; Who makes us the temple of God, and His house; Who intercedes for us, acting as our advocate and defender, dwelling in our bodies and sanctifying them for immortality. He it is who fights against the flesh: hence the flesh fights against the Spirit."

In a series of articles in a well-known denominational weekly, entitled "By This I Live . . . . ," a number of Christian ministers and laymen were invited to give their testimony. One of them, Douglas Brown, a lay leader

from Yorkshire, wrote about "The Indwelling Spirit."
The crisis in his Christian pilgrimage came when some
years ago in the course of conversation with one of his
clients (he is an estate agent) he happened to mention
that he was a preacher. The customer appeared greatly
surprised and said, "Well, I would never have suspected
it!" That incident led Douglas Brown to a serious re-
examination of his life and witness. It was evident that
his daily testimony was ineffective and his preaching was
not supported by an obviously dedicated life. Let him
continue his story himself: "What I needed was the indwelling Spirit of Christ. If I was 'to love my neighbour
as myself,' if I was to be what Dr. Barclay calls a 'winsome
Christian' witnessing to my Saviour more by my bearing
and deeds than by my words, then I must be able to say
with St. Paul, 'I live: and yet no longer I, but Christ
liveth in me.' After costly repentance and prayer I was
able 'to make a new beginning with Him who never fails
and whose promises 'Seek and ye shall find' and 'Ask
and it shall be given you' are as true today as ever."

II. We learn, too, that the Spirit of power is THE
IDENTIFYING SPIRIT (v.9b). The indwelling Spirit is the
means of the believer's union with Christ and also the
sign of it. Just as the royal standard above Buckingham
Palace indicates that the Queen is in residence, so the
mark of the Spirit bears witness to the fact that the King
of kings has taken up His abode within. The Spirit of
God, be it noted, is also the Spirit of Christ. It is His
function to make Christ real to our hearts. And unless
we do possess the Spirit, we cannot belong to Christ.

There is a certain restrained delicacy in the way Paul
puts it. He has said quite confidently: "But you are not
in the flesh, you are in the Spirit" (v.9a). Now he moves
from the actual to the hypothetical. If it should be that
anyone has not the Spirit, then it is evident that he cannot
be called a Christian at all. This is hypothetical so far as
the Romans are concerned, he has reason to hope: but

no doubt he has discovered from sad experience that it is not so everywhere. In Ephesus, for instance, there were some who supposed that they were Christians who had not so much as heard about the Holy Ghost (Acts 19:2). Now this is a most disturbing and challenging assertion here in the ninth verse. "If a man does not possess the Spirit of Christ, he is no Christian" (N.E.B.). There are no half measures about such a categorical declaration. Paul is making it unambiguously clear that the indwelling Spirit is not a kind of superadded luxury or optional extra. He is absolutely necessary to any knowledge of Christ at all.

If we go to buy a new car, we know that we can have either a standard or a de luxe model. The standard model has everything that is really essential. We could ride about in safety and comfort. But such further refinements as a fog lamp, a heater, a radio or a parking light are fitted as a special supplement. There are many people who think that the Christian experience of the Holy Spirit is something that is necessary only for those who aspire to the de luxe category. They somehow imagine that the plain, ordinary Christian need not bother about such a thing.

This verse should disabuse our minds of any misapprehension. It presents the Holy Spirit, not as an unessential refinement, but as a basic 'must.' "I never read this passage of Scripture in the presence of a Christian congregation," confessed C. H. Fowler, "without feeling I have in some way chopped down through every heart with a great broad axe. There is no whitewashing in this passage. 'If any man have not the Spirit of Christ, he is none of His.' Not: 'he will do tolerably well, but not quite so well as he might do;' not that he will get on after a fashion, and have quite a respectable entrance into the city of the great King, though he may not push quite so far towards the front as might have done if he had had the Spirit of the Lord Jesus. Not that at all: but, if any man have not the Spirit of Christ, there is not the remotest shadow of a chance for him: 'he is none of His'."

So far, then, from being the preoccupation only of those who are often regarded (however unjustifiably) as religious cranks, the Holy Spirit is the fundamental factor of all Christian life and experience. We are unable to believe as a Christian should without the Holy Spirit, for "no one can say 'Jesus is Lord' except by the Holy Spirit" (I Cor. 12:3). We are unable to live as a Christian should without the Holy Spirit, for as Matthew Henry has put it, "we cannot tread in His steps unless we have His Spirit."

If, then, possession by and of the Holy Spirit is the one thing needful to make us Christians, it will be true that Christians may be identified by this stamp. Writing to the Ephesians, Paul says that after they believed they were "sealed with the promised Holy Spirit" (Eph. 1:13); and again that they were sealed by the Holy Spirit of God "for the day of redemption" (Eph. 4:30). Now the seal in Roman use was a mark of ownership. A man would affix his personal seal to his goods when they were in transit. His clothes might bear a similar sign. Even his slaves could be branded with his seal. In each case it was an indication of proprietorship. It was, moreover, a common feature in primitive religion that the worshipper should be marked with the likeness of his pagan god. Herodotus describes a temple in Egypt at which a fugitive taking sanctuary might receive some physical incision which indicated that he now belonged to the god and was therefore not to be touched.

The Christian bears no external sign of his allegiance. His skin is not seared or tattooed. But nevertheless he carries with him an inward seal. The indwelling Spirit identifies us as belonging to Christ. When He is stamped upon our mind and heart then everybody will know whose we are and whom we serve. Unless we have the Spirit of Christ we cannot be His disciples, for the Spirit is the proof that we are His.

Here, then, is the test of Christianity. It is not membership of a church or subscription to a creed or advocacy of a cause that makes us Christians. It is not knowledge of the Scriptures or zeal in soul-winning or fidelity to the Gospel that makes us Christians. It is not kindness or gentleness or unselfishness or even love that makes us Christians. All these are fruits. They spring from the one basic necessity: to be Christ's we must have His Spirit. And if we are to conform to this biblical definition of a Christian, then the remedy will have to be applied within and not without. "I pray you," advised Dr. Campbell Morgan is one of his inspiring books, "attempt to correct the circumference of your life from the centre; do not attempt to correct the centre from the circumference – that is, do not attempt to correct your spirit by altering your habits. Correct your habits by an alteration of the spirit. And how is the spirit to be altered? Only by the true, whole-hearted unquestioning abandonment of your whole being to the Spirit of God will it be possible for you to have the Spirit of Christ."

III. We learn further that the Spirit of power is THE INVIGORATING SPIRIT (v.10). After speaking about the indwelling and identifying Spirit, Paul in the next two verses comes closer to his theme in this section: the power of the Spirit. In verse ten he talks about the vitalizing energy of the Holy Ghost as it affects us in this present life. Then in verse eleven he goes on to show how that same vitalizing energy is the means of our resurrection to life eternal.

All this, however, is governed by the crucial assumption at the outset of v.10. "But if Christ is in you." This is something Paul takes for granted, as in v.9. When he reaches his first benediction in 15:13 (there is a second and final one in 16:25–27) he is assured that the Roman Christians already experience the power of the Spirit which he prays may fill them with all joy and peace in believing. "I myself am satisfied about you, my brethren, that you yourselves are full of goodness."

"If Christ is in you:" that is another significant indwelling. In v.9. Paul has said that his readers live no longer in the flesh but in the Spirit, because the Spirit dwells in them. Then he has added that the Spirit is none other than the Spirit of Christ. So it is not surprising that now he should proceed to assume that Christ – the living, risen Lord Jesus – indwells them, for it is the function of the Spirit to bring about this mystical and mysterious union of the believer with his Saviour. Christ is only formed in our hearts by faith as the Holy Ghost is permitted to do His work within. That this is indeed an outcome of the Spirit's power is seen in Ephesians 3:16,17: "that according to the riches of his glory he may grant you to be strengthened with might through his Spirit in the inner man, and that Christ may dwell in your hearts through faith." The Comforter is also the Christopher – the Christ bearer – Who conveys the reality of Jesus to the soul. This is what our Lord Himself promised: "And I will pray the Father, and he shall give you another comforter (i.e. of the same kind that I have been) that he may abide with you for ever; even the Spirit of truth . . . He dwelleth with you, and shall be in you. I will not leave you comfortless: I will come to you" (John 14:16–18 A.V. cf.15:26).

What is the consequence of this further indwelling? The Authorized Version is preferable here in that it preserves the subtle discriminations involved, as we shall show later. "And if Christ be in you, the body is dead because of sin; but the Spirit is life because of righteousness." It would be better not to capitalize "spirit" here, for the allusion is not directly to the Holy Spirit, but to the regenerate human spirit indwelt by God, as in previous instances. In the section from v.5 to v.8 what is contrasted with flesh is spirit, and not the Holy Spirit. So here what is contrasted with the body is the spirit, not the Holy Spirit. But He is nevertheless the agent both of its creation and renewal and so there is a sense in which the believer's spirit is one with God's Spirit. The Holy Spirit can only operate through our spirits and our spirits only escape the fatal touch of death through the Holy Spirit. So, although the more recent versions are right in dropping the capital S in this verse, we must remember that *pneuma* here stands for the spirit of the Christian as filled by the Spirit of God. As Alford puts it, what is meant is "our spirit as possessed and penetrated by God's Spirit."

There is a dual and contrasted outcome of Christ's indwelling. In so far as the body is concerned – deadness: in so far as the spirit is concerned – life. And the reason is added in each case: because of sin, because of righteousness. Glance back to v.2 of this chapter. There, as we saw, the apostle declares that the law of the Spirit of life in Christ Jesus has made him free from the law of sin and death. In verses 3 and 4 he shows how we are freed from the law of sin. Now in verses 10 and 11 he shows how we are freed from the law of death. In verses 7 and 8 he had confirmed his statement in verse 6 that the mind of the flesh is death. Now he corroborates the opposite statement, that the mind of the Spirit is life.

The body, he says, is dead. The Scripture alludes to three kinds of death: one is *in* this life, another *at the end* of this life, and a third *after* this life. There is *spiritual* death. It is the condition of the sinner even in the midst of physical life (cf. Eph. 2:1; 4:18; Col. 2:13; Rom. 5:15; 6:13; I Tim. 5:6; I John 3:14). There is *natural* death, which terminates earthly life and separates soul from body (cf. Eccles. 8:8; Heb. 9:27; I Cor. 15:21,22; Acts 24:15). There is *eternal* death which is the fate of the wicked after judgment: it is the unending destruction which never reaches the point of annihilation (Matt. 10:28; Rom. 1:32; 6:23; II Thess. 1:9; Rev. 2:11; 20:14; 21:8). It is quite evident that Paul is speaking here in Romans 8:10 only of natural death. Believers are raised in this life from the death of sin and at the latter day they will be spared what Scripture calls the second or eternal death. But everybody (literally every body) must die. "The dust returns to the earth as it was" (Eccles. 12:7). The soul survives to await its partner the resurrected body at the end. But the body cannot escape corruption. So, even now, whilst we are living in it, the body is doomed to die. It bears the sentence of death upon it. In this respect, the Christian's body is in the same case as that of the unbeliever.

> *Golden lads and girls all must,*
> *As chimney-sweepers, come to dust.*

The doom of the body is due to sin that entered the world in Adam. The curse of God fell upon our first ancestor in the shape of mortality. "You are dust, and to dust you shall return" (Gen. 3:19). Paul has already made that plain in Romans 5:12–21. Sin came into the world through one man and death by sin. From Adam to Christ sin reigned by death, and still does in those who prefer to live in Adam rather than in Christ.

On the other hand, Paul continues, the spirit is life. And this is because of righteousness. Death rules through sin: life prevails through sin's opposite. This righteousness is clearly not human. Nothing that man can do of his own accord can gain him life. It is the righteousness of Christ that opens the life gate that all may go in who believe.

Observe the precise form of this balanced statement. The minute accuracy of Scripture is apparent here. Paul does not say, as we might expect, that the body is *dead* and the spirit is *alive* (though the Revised Standard Version overlooks the difference and renders it thus). Neither does he say that the body is *death* and the spirit *life*. Either of these declarations would have satisfied the canons of syntax, but they would not have conveyed the exact truth of God. What the inspired Word tells us here is that the body is *dead* and the spirit is *life*. An adjective is attached to the body, but a noun to the spirit, and we must not set aside the deliberate distinction. The New English Bible hits it off admirably: "But if Christ is dwelling in you, then although the body is a dead thing because you sinned, yet the spirit is life itself because you have been justified." The body is not death, that is, in a state of

everlasting death: it is only dead, and will live again.
And the spirit is not merely alive or living, which might
imply a consequent death. It is life, for "he who has the
Son has life" (I John 5:12). It comes, of course, from the
life-giving Spirit.

IV. We learn finally that the Spirit of power is THE
IMMORTALIZING SPIRIT (v.11). Already the believer possesses
eternal life in Christ. At the moment of natural death his
body is consigned to the grave, but his soul lives on. Yet
even the death of the body is only temporary. It will be
raised from the tomb and clothed with immortality.
And the agent of resurrection, as in the prototype of Easter,
is the Holy Spirit. This, then, is what has been called
"the Gospel for the body."

This verse repays the closest examination. Every word
has its own importance. Once again as in v.10, the apostle
assumes that his readers are indwelt by the Spirit – now:
"if the Spirit of him who raised Jesus from the dead *dwells*
in you." The tense is present, as is the indwelling. And
this abiding of the Spirit within is the token and pledge
of eventual immortality. The body is mortal because of
sin: but through the Holy Spirit the soul will survive the
shock of death and, through the same Spirit, the body
itself will be raised at the latter day and put on immortality,
too, in its glorified state. We are not surprised to learn
that this is a miracle in which all three Divine persons
cooperate. It is a Trinitarian achievement. "The Spirit
(the third person) of him (the first person) who raised
Jesus (the second person) from the dead." Our Lord is
referred to first as Jesus to emphasize that it was a man
who was raised to life by the Spirit of God on that amazing
Easter morning. There is the earnest of our own resurrection. "Made like Him, like Him we rise." But when
the event is mentioned a second time, our Lord is called
Christ. This is His official title as Messiah. It is clearly
indicated that only as the uniquely begotten Son of the
Father is He equipped to be the prince and pioneer of

life. He was the first to rise from the dead, and this by virtue of His Divine Sonship.

The distinction between our Lord's resurrection and ours is also brought out by the respective verbs employed. It is said that God "raised Jesus from the dead." That means simply to awaken from sleep. It is used of the disciples rousing the Master as He slept in the stern of the ship whilst the storm raged around Him (Mark 4:38). It is used when the angel appeared to Peter in prison, slapped him and said, "Get up quickly" (Acts 12:7). This is all that was needed to bring Christ back from Hades on the first glad Easter day. But another verb altogether is employed to describe the resurrection of believers. They are to be given life or quickened. The word is *zōopoieō* – to make alive or cause to live. This is different from what the Father did in raising the Son. It is what He will do in virtue of our Lord's resurrection (John 5:21; I Cor. 15:45). The expression implies, moreover, something beyond rising from the grave. It suggests the communication to the body of that life of which Christ is the source and the Spirit the giver. So we read in I Corinthians 15:22: "For as in Adam all die, so also in Christ shall all be made alive."

Here, then, the power of the Spirit is demonstrated at its most remarkable level. The resurrection of Christ and the consequent resurrection of the believing dead to life immortal, is the crowning work of the Spirit. In an age which worships power, we do well to remind ourselves that all the incredible energies locked up in the atom are as nothing and less than nothing compared with the supernatural might that brought back Jesus from the dead and will one day quicken and transform our mortal bodies that they may be conformed to Christ's own glorious body.

The immediate reference of this verse then, is to the ultimate achievement of the Spirit in making us fit for heaven by raising and renewing the body of our humiliation. But, as Calvin rightly reminds us, we cannot divorce this from "the continued operation of the Spirit, which, extinguishing by degrees the remainder of the fleshly mind, restores in us celestial life." Pardon and holiness and heaven are interlinked. The one brings us to the other.

> *The holy to the holiest leads,*
> *From thence our spirits rise,*
> *And he that in Thy statutes treads*
> *Shall meet Thee in the skies.*

Verses 12 and 13 represent Paul's winding up of the whole matter from v.5 onwards. "So then" is resumptive. It gathers up the threads of the previous argument. In view of all this, Paul says, we owe a duty, or are under an obligation, not to the flesh, for that way leads to death – spiritual as well as physical. We should expect that the apostle would go on to say "but to the Spirit," and this we must take to be in his mind before the remainder of v.13. The body is already doomed to death, but in the life of the sanctified believer, even its *deeds* are done away as they are crucified with Christ. As Karl Barth says, "Life emerges at the point of mortification." When self dies, Christ lives and holiness begins. That is why each believer must attend what Oswald Chambers used to call "a white funeral," when self is buried without a tear of regret or a mourning weed, so that Christ may reign supreme. Only so shall we live now and live hereafter. The testimony to cherish is that of Paul himself: "I have been crucified with Christ; it is no longer I who live, but Christ who lives in me" (Gal. 2:20).

CHAPTER FIVE

THE GUIDANCE OF THE SPIRIT

WHEN THAT GRAND OLD MAN OF METHODISM, Dr. John Scott Lidgett, came to write his autobiography towards the end of his exceptionally long ministry, he choose an arresting title. It was typical of the man and summed up what he really felt about all his many years of Christian service. He looked down the corridor of time and then took up his pen and wrote this at the head of his narrative: "My Guided Life." That was a testimony in itself. He bore witness to the fact that he had been always aware that God was directing his steps. He had an overwhelming sense that the Divine hand had steered him along his course. For him, guidance was one of the determinative realities of his experience.

Not everyone feels that. Not everyone accepts the possibility of such supervision. There are some who argue that life is an aimless farce – "a long fool's errand to the grave," as A. E. Housman had it. All we can do, they say, is to muddle along as best we can. No thread of purpose can be discerned amid the jumble of circumstance. We merely wander about the stage of existence for a few brief and empty years, and then make our inconspicuous and inconsequential exit. Others are convinced that we are all in the relentless grip of an inexorable fate. We have no part at all in our own destiny. We are like so many clock-work dolls, wound up by some mysterious hand and left to "click-clack off their pre-adjusted laws," as Thomas Hardy cynically expressed it. Obviously, those who regard life like this – either as a futile drift or a forced march of automatons, can find no room for the Christian conception of guidance from a loving Father, God.

But that, nevertheless, is the Christian view, even though not all Christians are in fact exploring to the full the rich possibilities of the God-controlled life. The Christian is a man who believes in Divine guidance. This is more than an opinion he has formed: he receives his assurance from revelation. The Bible firmly offers the promise of unerring direction. When Isaiah declares, (after setting out the necessary conditions) "And the Lord will guide you continually" (Isa. 58:11), he is reiterating one of the basic undertakings of Scripture. "The idea of steadfast providential guidance," according to T. G. Selby, "is one of the fixed polar ideas of both the Old and New Testament." Whilst the natural man, therefore, may continue to question the phenomenon of spiritual control, the believer cannot remain in uncertainty, for this is something he lives by every day. He can no more doubt the guidance of God than he can doubt his own existence. He recognises what Wordsworth described as "a peculiar grace, a leading from above, a something given."

According to the Bible, the guidance of God is communicated to the believer by the Holy Spirit. It is His specific function to direct us along God's chosen way. Before we consider the leading of the Spirit as presented to us in the fourteenth verse of Romans Eight, let us search the Scriptures in general so as to discover what is the teaching of the Word on this vital subject. The evidence has been collected most helpfully by Dr. René Pache in his fine book on *The Person and Work of the Holy Spirit*, and we shall be availing ourselves of his diligence in what follows. In the chapter which handles this theme Dr. Pache has spoken about the teaching office of the Spirit and, in a sense, this is part of His guidance, for our Lord promised that the Comforter would guide into all truth (John 14:26; 16:13). But He not only brings an understanding of Scriptural revelation to the believer's heart and mind: He also leads step by step those who put their trust in God. The guidance of the Spirit relates to the practical business of daily living. It is possible to enjoy explicit instruction at every point in our pilgrimage. Samuel Chadwick firmly believed that. "The humblest followers of Jesus," he wrote, "may know the Divine will at first hand. It is every man's privilege to be fully assured in the will of God. The Divine attention to detail is amazing. Nothing is too trivial for omniscience. Come straight to God. Lay all questions naked before Him and He will make it plain to you what is His will."

Turning to the Scriptures, then, we shall consider four aspects of the Spirit's guidance. Each will lend its illumination to this verse in which Paul announces that "all who are led by the Spirit of God are sons of God."

I. First we must enquire THE TIME OF THE SPIRIT'S GUIDANCE. When does He guide? And the only adequate answer to that query is, "Always, if we let Him." Failure is only on our side, never on His. We may not hear His messages if sin is blocking the line, but those messages are constantly being sent out. It might be that a ship at sea would drift off course because the radio operator had been inattentive to his duty. The message was being transmitted: the imperfection lay at the receiving end.

The most serious interference is sin. We cannot hope to benefit by God's help if we persist in known transgression. However small the offence may seem to us, it can shut us off from God and prevent us from hearing His voice. Some years ago, when one of the great underwater cables was being laid across the Atlantic, after many hundreds of miles had been covered, a serious fault was found in one of the sections. The current became faint, the needle reactions uncertain and the testing message sent from the shore end from time to time quite unintelligible. The fault was localized, the section in which it occurred taken up and at last the cause was revealed. One small shred of wire had dropped into the insulating coat when the cable was being prepared. It had forced its way through the coat and earthed the current. Communication was destroyed over hundreds of miles because of one tiny piece of wire. In the same way, one apparently insignificant sin can prevent us from hearing God's message and receiving His guidance through the Spirit. Cleansing is the prerequisite of communion. But when we are right with God, then we may look for His lead at all times. Return to the verse that was quoted from Isaiah earlier and weigh the meaning of the adverb: "And the Lord will guide you *continually*" (Isa. 58:11).

The Book of Acts will provide us with some striking instances of when the Spirit guides. It is entitled "The Acts of the Apostles," but it is really the acts of the Holy Spirit through the apostles that are recorded. In 8:29 we learn that while Philip was walking on the desert road to Gaza and came upon the Ethiopian eunuch reading from the Scriptures as he rode, the Spirit told him: "Go up and join this chariot." In 10:19,20 when Peter was puzzled by a vision that had appeared to him and was at a loss to interpret it, the Spirit said to him: "Behold, three men are looking for you. Rise and go down, and accompany them without hesitation; for I have sent them." In 13:2–4 Barnabas and Paul were separated and sent out on their pioneer missionary journey by the Spirit. But perhaps the most notable instance occurs in 16:6,7. Previously we have read how the Spirit led on. Here He restrains. Paul, Silas and Timothy had made a tour of Phrygia and Galatia. They evidently planned to push further into Asia Minor, but the unmistakeable veto of the Spirit prevented them. They were "forbidden by the Holy Spirit to speak the word in Asia." The verb means to hinder, to hold back, to stand in the way. So forcible was the intervention of the Spirit that it had the effect of flinging a barrier across the road into the Asian province. In the next verse we read that "when they had come opposite Mysia, they attempted to go into Bithynia." Their route southwards had been stopped, so now they headed north into another Roman province.

The verb here means that they made an effort or endeavoured to turn into Bithynia. But once again they were frustrated. The Spirit would not allow them. He refused to let them, or let them alone (so the word could mean) in peace of mind. They were on the wrong road and were told so. In the Nelson *Atlas of the Bible* – a magnificent production indeed – a broken blue line indicates that this was one of the "journeys planned but thwarted" – not by human opposition but by the Spirit's prohibition. The Revised Standard Version, following the Revised Version and the best textual readings here, says that it was "the Spirit of Jesus" who forbade them. The guidance of the Spirit was the guidance of Christ Himself. It was as if the Lord stood in the path and held up His hand to halt their entry. So they turned right round and headed for Troy. There it was that God spoke to Paul through a vision in which he saw that mysterious man of Macedonia pleading for help. Thus the message of life was first brought to Europe – that was the epoch-making outcome of this instance of the Spirit's guidance. There was no uncertainty now. Paul and his companions immediately "sought to go on into Macedonia, concluding that God had called us to preach the Gospel to them" (v.10). This joyful compliance with the Spirit's leading was followed by a markedly successful mission in Philippi.

The final references in Acts all have to do with Paul's visit to Jerusalem. In 19:21 Luke tells us that the apostle "resolved in the Spirit to pass through Macedonia and Achaia and go to Jerusalem," intending then to make for Rome. In 20:22 he informed the Ephesian elders: "And now, behold, I am going to Jerusalem, bound in the Spirit, not knowing what shall befall me there; except that the Holy Spirit testifies to me in every city that imprisonment and afflictions await me." This forecast of tribulation ahead was confirmed by the prophet Agabus in 21:11 as "he took Paul's girdle and bound his own feet and hands, and said, 'Thus says the Holy Spirit, So shall the Jews at Jerusalem bind the man who owns this

girdle and deliver him into the hands of the Gentiles'."
The apostle, however, refused to be deterred and pursued
his providential way to the sacred city. There he was
afforded an opportunity, through his arrest, to give his
testimony to the mob. Like Israel in the wilderness, Paul
was led in to be led out. From the barracks in Jerusalem
he was to be taken by a devious route, fraught with hazards,
to his final confinement in Rome. Before his departure
he was given a last assurance that his steps were still being
ordered by the Lord. The glorified Saviour Himself
stood by him in his cell and said: "Take courage, for as
you have testified about me at Jerusalem, so you must
bear witness also at Rome" (23:11). "This is the indication," commented Dr. Elder Cumming, "that 'the purpose
of the Spirit' (19:21) was to be carried out, and that
he would be 'led' to the end."

The time of the Spirit's guidance, then, is always, and
especially in the hour of crisis and decision. This impressive evidence from Acts is sufficient to convince us
that God will superintend every step of the Christian
way. All the milestones are known to Him and He will
point the path. "If encouraged on our part," states the
writer just quoted, "the leading of the Spirit will distinctly
increase and grow into a very definite and blessed habit
of the soul." That is what God intends for His children.
Reliance on His direction is to be habitual.

II. Next we must identify THE RECIPIENTS OF THE
SPIRIT'S GUIDANCE. It may have been noticed that the
cases quoted from Acts all concerned evangelists. They
had to do with the missionary work of the Church. We
must not, however, be tempted to imagine that the guidance
of the Spirit is therefore reserved for a special class of
Christians who are doing a particular type of work. The
fact of the matter is that in the primitive Church every
member was an evangelist. Some went off on tours, like
Paul and Barnabas and Silas and Timothy. Others stayed
at home and witnessed where they were. But all believers

were missionaries. A non-propagating Christian would have been considered a contradiction in terms. All had received the Spirit and so "you shall be my witnesses" (Acts 1:8) was fulfilled in them as well as in the twelve.

That is the plain implication of this 14th verse of Romans Eight: "All who follow the leading of God's Spirit are God's own sons" (Phillips). If they are indeed sons, they will do their Father's bidding, as Christ Himself did without intermission. God requires that His children should bear His name to the nations. That was the task of the old Israel and will be again. It is also the task of the Church in the present age. "Go therefore and make disciples of all nations, baptizing them in the name of the Father and of the Son and of the Holy Spirit, teaching them to observe all that I have commanded you; and lo, I am with you always, to the close of the age" (Matt. 28:19,20). It is through the Holy Spirit that Christ fulfils that promise and under the urge of the same Spirit that believers will pursue the evangelistic commission.

"It were good that this text were written in letters of gold," declared Luther, referring to Romans 8:14, "so admirable is it, and full of comfort." It is, indeed, the classical Scripture verse dealing with the Spirit's guidance. The only other which speaks in similar terms is Galatians 5:18. There Paul has been describing the Christian's walk in the Spirit and contrasting it, as in Romans Eight, with the life of the flesh. "But if you are led by the Spirit," he adds, "you are not under the law." Here in Romans 8:14 there is no "if." There have been some (vv.9, 10, 11, 13), but now they are all left behind. This is a ringing affirmation to assure us that without any sort of doubt those who are guided by the Spirit are indeed God's sons.

There is a twofold truth in this verse. It can be read backwards and forwards. It is reversible. Those who are led by the Spirit are the sons of God. And we can put it the other way round and still find it to be true. It is the sons of God who are led by the Spirit. In fact, it would seem that this is what Paul is seeking primarily to say.

Nowhere in the Bible is the Spirit's guidance given to the unconverted. How could He possibly lead those who resist Him and disallow His entrance into their hearts?

It is the sons of God who are the recipients of the Spirit's guidance. And it is the Spirit who makes them sons. We are not naturally sons of God. By sin we have forfeited our inheritance at creation. The Jews might boast that they had Abraham for their father, but our Lord roundly told them that they were children of the devil (John 8:44). Christ nowhere treats unbelievers as sons of God. It is an informative straw in the wind that in his New Testament theology Professor A. M. Hunter is at pains to dispel any such notion. "Jesus did *not* preach God as Father to the multitudes. On his lips the Fatherhood of God was not a theological commonplace. He spoke of God as Father only to His disciples in private." And again: "Jesus did *not* teach God's universal Fatherhood. He spoke of God as His own Father, and taught that others might become His sons. But for this high privilege they must become debtors to Himself. Not sons of God by nature, they might become sons by grace. The Johannine saying, 'No one comes to the Father, but by me' (14:6) is confirmed by the Synoptic, 'And no one knows the Father except the Son and anyone to whom the Son chooses to reveal him' (Matt. 11:27; Luke 10:27)."

In order, then, that we may become sons of God, we have to be born again, and this, of course, is a work of the Spirit. He so applies the effective benefits of our Lord's redemptive death that we are delivered from the curse of Adam's sin and from bondage to the law so that we might enjoy the glorious liberty of the sons of God. "It is vain for man to look with pride upon the surviving traces of the sonship which took its rise in an original creation," wrote T. G. Selby, "for the rights and privileges of that sonship have been lost, and can never be brought back by purely natural methods and evolutions. To make the name mean anything but shame, retrogression, a curse, it needs that great miracle which is to the Jews a stumbling-block, and to the Greeks foolishness. Our elder Brother takes away the bar between God and His apostate sons, and the privileges they thenceforth enjoy, they enjoy through their union with Jesus Christ alone. We are in no valid sense members of a divine family by our descent from Adam, who was at first 'the son of God,' but by Christ, who brings us back into the household, and makes His Father our Father once more."

Paul develops this line more fully in the next verse, as we shall be seeing. But he prepares the way here by being careful to speak of Spirit-led believers as sons rather than as children. The Greek noun *teknon*, a child, means strictly that which is begotten physically, like the Scottish 'bairn.' But *huios*, a son, has to do with position, or status. It is possible to become a son by adoption, but a child is only so by birth. Humanly speaking, adoption supplies the lack of children. No one can at one and the same time be both a trueborn child and an adopted son in relation to one father. But in the realm of the Spirit, what is impossible with men becomes wonderfully possible with God. The Christian is both a child by new birth and a son by adoption. And each is the work of the Spirit. It is of the latter that Paul is proposing to treat in verse 15, so he selects the appropriate title by way of introduction. We shall be entering into fuller detail in the next study. It is sufficient to note now that it is the sons of God who are favoured with His direction. They are the recipients of the Spirit's guidance.

III. Now we must investigate THE MANNER OF THE SPIRIT'S GUIDANCE. What are the means and methods He employs? That question requires us to look more closely at the word here rendered as "led." It is really quite a simple one from the verb *agō*. It signifies to guide, to show the way, to bring on the way and sometimes even to impel. That is why the New English Bible has "moved."

An examination of its occurrences will help us to grasp its meaning more fully. No form of Bible study is more profitable than this coverage in depth as we compare Scripture with Scripture and allow the Word to be its own interpreter. This same verb to lead is used in John 10:16 of the shepherd bringing his sheep into the fold (as he has previously led them out, v.3), and that is a figure we should keep in mind throughout. For variations on this theme, if we may borrow an expression from the realm of music, it is instructive to set side by side the synoptic accounts of our Lord's temptation in the wilderness. In Luke 4:1 this same word *agō* is employed – Jesus "was *led* by the Spirit." Matthew 4:1 has the same word with the prefix *ana*—up, or upwards. "Then Jesus was *led up* by the Spirit into the wilderness." The first has to do with the Spirit's action on the soul of Christ which induced Him to go. The second has to do with the actual direction of the Spirit during His journey from the Jordan, below sea level, up to the waste land above. Some commentators wonder whether the meaning might even be that our Lord was snatched away as Ezekiel was in the Old Testament (Ezek. 11:1) and Philip in the New (Acts 8:39). That is why the New English Bible has "led away" in Matthew 4:1, to allow of both possibilities. If the latter is correct, it suggests something overwhelmingly forceful. This would fit what Mark gives us in his very striking version: "The Spirit immediately *drove him out* into the wilderness" (Mark 1:12). The verb *ekballō* means to cast out, to expel. It is the normal one to describe how our Lord exorcised demons. It is also applied in Mark 9:47 to the removal of an eye, in Mark 11:15 to the ejection of those who desecrated the temple with their commercialization and in Mark 12:8 to the expulsion of the heir from the vineyard. "Used here with *euthus* (immediately)," comments Dr. Vincent Taylor on Mark 1:12, "the verb appears to indicate strong, if not violent propulsion." It is perhaps with this parallel in mind that Karl Barth interprets Romans 8:14 as meaning "clutched by the truth."

We might therefore conclude that, pressed to its fullest

limit, the word implies controlled guidance. It suggests that the believer is in the grip of the Spirit. "It has stamped upon it," observed B. B. Warfield, "the conception of the exertion of a power of control over the actions of its subject, which the strength of the led one is insufficient to withstand." We find many occurrences in the New Testament which underline this element of compulsion. It is used, for example, of leading animals, as when on the first Palm Sunday, our Lord sent His disciples to locate the ass and her colt, and commanded them to untie them and *bring* them to Him (Matt. 21:2,7); or as when Isaiah declares, in the Scripture which was being read by the Ethiopian eunuch when Philip climbed into his chariot, "As a sheep *led* to the slaughter, or a lamb before its shearer is dumb, so he opens not his mouth" (Acts 8:32; Isa. 53:7). It is applied to the conveyance of sick folk, who are not in a fit state to determine their own movements: as when in Luke 4:40 the sufferers were *brought* at sunset to the Lord, or in Luke 10:34 the Good Samaritan set the wounded traveller on his own beast and *brought* him to an inn and took care of him, or in Luke 18:40 when Jesus commanded the blind man of Jericho to be *brought* to Him (cf. John 9:13).

It is most commonly used to describe the enforced movements of prisoners: in John 8:3 the woman taken in adultery was dragged unwillingly to Jesus; in Luke 23:1 the crowd led Jesus to Pilate: in John 18:13 Jesus was led first to Annas: then in John 18:28 He was led from the palace of Caiaphas to the Praetorium; in John 19:13 Pilate brought Him out to the Pavement; in Luke 23:32 He was led away to the place of crucifixion. In Acts 6:12 Stephen was seized and brought before the Council; in Acts 9:2 Saul was supplied with letters to the synagogues at Damascus "so that if he found any belonging to the Way, men or women, he might bring them bound to Jerusalem" (cf. v.21); in Acts 18:12 the Jews made a concerted attack on Paul and hauled him before the tribunal of the proconsul Gallio; in Acts 21:34 the Roman

tribune in Jerusalem, unable to make head or tail of
what the Jewish mob wanted to do with Paul, ordered
him to be brought into the barracks; in Acts 23:10 he
did the same again and in v.31 Paul was removed by a
squad to Antipatris; in Acts 25:6 Festus arriving in state
at Caesarea ordered Paul to be brought and later he was
similarly summoned before Agrippa. "In a word," concludes Warfield, who cites many of these instances, "though
the term may, of course, sometimes be used when the
idea of force retires somewhat into the background,
and is commonly so used when it is transferred from external
compulsion to internal influence – as, for example, when
we are told that Barnabas took Paul and led him to the
apostles (Acts 9:37), and that Andrew led Simon to
Jesus (John 1:42) – yet the proper meaning of the word
includes the idea of control, and the implication of pre-
vailing determination of action never leaves it."

The many usages of this verb "to lead" reveal how the
Spirit guides the sons of God. His manner is not only by
suggestion but even more by compulsion. He does more
than draw from without: He drives from within. That is
the glad testimony of those who have received the fulness
of the Spirit. They are conscious of being projected on
their course by the impetus of the Spirit. The Christian
is jet-propelled. The indwelling Spirit urges him on his
God-appointed way. He acknowledges with the prophet
Jeremiah "that it is not in man who walks to direct his
steps" (Jer. 10:23), and is content to be led of the Spirit.

IV.   As we take leave of this section, we must ascertain
THE DIRECTION OF THE SPIRIT'S GUIDANCE. Where will He
lead the sons of God? We can rest assured that those who
place themselves under His superintendence will be
guided solely along the line of God's good purpose. That
purpose can be summed up in a single word: holiness.
All that God designs for the believer is contained in that
inclusive term. "For this is the will of God, your sanctification" (I Thess. 4:3).

Holiness, then, is not only a calling (II Thess. 1:11): it is an election. It is the "good pleasure of His goodness" or, as Phillips has it, the effecting in us of "all that His goodness desires to do." From before the foundation of the world God has determined to make His people holy. Sanctification is no afterthought. It is the agelong objective of Him who created us to the praise of His glory. Believers have been "chosen and destined by God the Father and sanctified by the Spirit for obedience to Jesus Christ and for sprinkling with His blood (I Pet. 1:2). "God chose you from the beginning," Paul informs the Thessalonians, "to be saved through sanctification by the Spirit and belief in the truth" (II Thess. 2:13).

The appointed agent of sanctification is the Holy Spirit. Man cannot make himself holy. It is only "the God of peace himself" who can "sanctify us wholly" so that our "spirit and soul and body be kept sound and blameless at the coming of our Lord Jesus Christ" (I Thess. 5:23). But this He achieves through the Spirit. Sanctification is the specific work of Him who leads the sons of God. The guidance of the Spirit is the passport to holiness.

The mode of the Spirit's operation as He conducts the Christian towards this all-embracing goal is wrapped in mystery. Some discerning comments of Professor John Murray are apposite to this consideration. "While we must not do prejudice to the fact that the Spirit's work in our hearts reflects itself in our awareness and consciousness," he writes, "while we must not relegate sanctification to the realm of the subconscious and fail to recognize that sanctification draws within its orbit the whole field of conscious activity on our part, yet we must also appreciate the fact that there is an agency on the part of the Holy Spirit that far surpasses analysis or introspection on our part. The effects of this constant and uninterrupted agency come within the scope of our consciousness in understanding, feeling, and will. But we must not suppose that the measure of our understanding or experience is the measure of the Spirit's working. In every distinct and particular movement of the believer in the way of holiness there is an energizing activity of the Holy Spirit, and when we try to discover what the mode of that exercise of his grace and power is we realize how far we are from being able to diagnose the secret workings of the Spirit."

There is another word in the New Testament derived from *agō*, to lead. The similarity can be detected in the form of it. It is *prosagōge*. In the Authorized Version it is translated as "access." Paul has used it in Romans 5:2 where he says that it is through Christ that he and his readers "have been allowed to enter the sphere of God's grace, where we now stand" (N.E.B.). It occurs again in Ephesians 2:18 where we are told that through Christ both Jews and Gentiles have access to the Father in the one Spirit. That is the direction of the Spirit's guidance. No doubt Paul is conjuring up a picture here. In the ancient world a king was heavily guarded, not only by his retinue of soldiers, but also by the red tape of officialdom. As a result, it was extremely difficult, if not altogether impossible, to gain an entrée into his presence. Usually he had a trusted court official whose job it was to determine who could be granted a royal audience. His title was the *prosagōgeus* or introducer.

That is the office of the Holy Spirit. He will lead us into the presence of the King of kings. He is the Divine Introducer who brings us right to the throne of the Father. And that is where holiness begins and grows. Only those who constantly abide under the shadow of the Almighty, whose lives are continually hid with Christ in God, will receive the stamp of sanctity. It is the son who is ever with his father who displays the family features, in terms of character even more than physical affinity. Union with God brings likeness to God. Holiness is simply the reflected beauty of the Lord Himself. "And we all, with unveiled face, beholding the glory of the Lord, are being changed into his likeness from one degree of glory to another; for this comes from the Lord who is the Spirit" (II Cor. 3:18).

CHAPTER SIX

THE ADOPTION OF THE SPIRIT

THE GREAT SWISS PROTESTANT BIBLE COMMENTATOR, F. L. Godet, used to describe Romans as the cathedral of Christian truth. There is a spacious grandeur about it which makes the comparison peculiarly apt. It is large enough to walk about in, with heights that soar beyond our range of vision and windows which let in the light of heaven to illuminate the place where we kneel in reverent submission to God.

The theme which next engages our attention is a lofty one indeed. Adolf Harnack once declared that there is no subject to graver importance for a man than his relation to God, and that everything depends upon it. The fifteenth verse of Romans Eight which we now reach deals with that all important matter. It speaks of what man may become through the work of the Spirit. He can enter into filial communion with God his Father. He can rejoice in all the privileges of sonship. The thought of the previous verse is carried forward. There this sonship of believers was linked with the guidance of the Spirit. It is the sons of God who are led by the Spirit and it is into the experience of sonship in its increasing fulness that the Spirit leads. The 15th verse looks more closely at that experience and, employing a method already familiar to us from an earlier section (5-8), contrasts it with its opposite.

The spirit of adoption is set over against the spirit of bondage. There is, in fact, a threefold contradistinction, and we may lay it out thus, for the sake of clarity:—

75

The spirit of bondage – of a slave – of fear.

The spirit of adoption – of a son – of faith.

Bondage, slavery and fear are marked off from adoption, sonship and faith. But, having analysed the verse in this way, we shall proceed to expound it with the further addition of what we call the spirit of recognition. This stands on the same side of the contrast as the spirit of adoption and represents its expression. Throughout spirit will be spelt with a small "s." As in vv.5 and 6 and again in v.10, the contrast is kept on the human level. But we shall also recall that God's Spirit is the efficient cause of all that the believer's spirit does, so that actions are identical. The third person of the blessed Trinity is indeed the Spirit of adoption, but what is alluded to here is His operation in that capacity viewed from the angle of the son who benefits by His intervention.

I. But first we are confronted by THE SPIRIT OF BONDAGE AND THE HERITAGE OF FEARFULNESS. Spirit can be used in Scripture both in a good sense and in a bad sense. In the good sense it may refer to the Holy Spirit Himself or, if the context is clearly human, it may indicate the renewed nature of the Christian man, as it does in the second half of this 15th verse and again in the second half of the 16th verse.

But spirit may be used in Scripture in a bad sense too. In Isaiah 19:14 from the oracle on Egypt we read: "The Lord has mingled within her a spirit of confusion;" and again in Isaiah 29:10: "For the Lord has poured upon you a spirit of deep sleep, and has closed your eyes, the prophets, and covered your heads, the seers." So here in the first part of Romans 8:15 spirit is used in a bad sense to describe the bondage of sin and law. It is not necessarily suggested that there is a personal spirit of bondage – and indeed only those who fail to recognize that the spirit of adoption mentioned in the corresponding phrase is not the Holy Spirit would feel the need to press such an interpretation. The spirit of bondage, then, is not an external entity, although it is governed by the Evil One just as the spirit of adoption in the regenerate is governed by the Holy One of God. Nor as Kingsley Barrett surmises, is this simply "a rhetorical formation," for that could be taken to mean that it is without substance. It is simply the unredeemed human *pneuma*.

All who are not dead to the law, and know of no way to escape the Divine displeasure but by striving to obey it, are included as victims under the spirit of bondage. They serve in the oldness of the letter, not in newness of spirit. For, so far from fulfilling the demands of the law, they realize how lamentably short they fall of its standards. The law presents them with an unattainable ideal. In vainly endeavouring to meet its inflexible requirements, they fall prey to frustration and despair. Bondage to the law is an aspect of bondage to sin, for the one brings the consciousness of the other. That had been Paul's own experience, as he tells us in the autobiographical Seventh Chapter. "If it had not been for the law, I should not have known sin. I should not have known what it is to covet if the law had not said, 'You shall not covet.' But sin, finding opportunity in the commandment, wrought in me all kinds of covetousness. Apart from the law, sin lies dead. I was once alive apart from the law, but when the commandment came, sin revived and I died; the very commandment which promised life proved to be death to me" (Rom. 7:7–10).

This servile dread of punishment characterizes the slave-spirit. Men cringe before God as under the lash of a stern taskmaster. He appears only as a heartless tyrant. The slave obeys his owner from fear, not from love or gratitude. He knows that his master is stronger than he is: he is afraid of punishment and so he obeys, not willingly and gladly, but by compulsion.

The spirit of bondage is accurately depicted in our Lord's parable of the pounds (Luke 19:11–27). This is one of the striking tales that Jesus told. It has to do with a nobleman who went off to a distant land to claim a kingdom – a sidelong reference to Archelaus, who journeyed to Rome in 4 B.C. to secure his share of the kingship under the will of Herod the Great. He called together his ten slaves and entrusted ten pounds to them, telling them to trade profitably until his return. When he came back, he wanted to know how much each slave had gained by his trading. One had turned his pound into ten: another into five; and each received appropriate commendation and reward. But a third came to his master and said: "Here is your pound, sir; I kept it put away in a handker-chief. I was afraid of you, because you are a hard man; you draw out what you never put in and reap what you did not sow" (vv.20,21 N.E.B.). Here is the slave-spirit personified. This man's overcautious policy stemmed from his misinterpretation of his master's character. The first two servants refused to be cramped by their status and acted like free men. But this fearful, creeping figure failed to seize the opportunity that was given him to prove himself something more than a serf. Even if his estimate of his owner's nature had been accurate, there would still have been no justification for his timidity. But the reply of the nobleman rather confirms the view that he was not quite such a martinet as the spineless slave made out. "You rascal! I will judge you by your own words. You knew, did you, that I am a hard man, that I draw out what I never put in, and reap what I did not sow? Then why did you not put my money on deposit, and I could have claimed it with interest when I came back?" (vv.22, 23 N.E.B.). The unfortunate man had only succeeded in adding insult to injury, and was thus justly deprived of the pound he had so miserably failed to improve.

This, then, is the spirit of bondage which Paul refers to here in Romans 8:15. In its subjection to sin and law it fails to recognize a gracious God. What Christians say about His Fatherhood seems incomprehensible to such a craven outlook. Paul has handled the same theme previously in Galatians – which in a number of points appears like a draft copy of Romans. In Galatians 4:21–26 the apostle compares the two covenants, namely the law from Mount Sinai and the Gospel from Jerusalem. The one from Sinai, he says, engenders bondage, like Hagar; but Jerusalem, which is above, is free, the mother of all believers, and her offspring are like Isaac, children of promise.

The spirit of bondage is received "to fall back into fear." That is its fatal heritage and those who are under its domination enter into it. A double opposition is involved, as Haldane brings out: the one of man's state before and after his regeneration: the other of the Old Testament and the New. Before his new birth, a man who knows he is a sinner must be apprehensive of punishment since he has not taken advantage of the remedy provided in Christ for the remission of sins. This is only true of those who have been awakened. The great majority live in profane security, with callous consciences, oblivious to their desperate state. But God in His mercy often impresses the fear of death and the punishment of sin upon those whom he wills to lead to the knowledge of His salvation. Then, when they are born again, that servile fear becomes a filial fear proceeding from love. "In this is love perfected with us, that we may have confidence in the day of judgment, because as he is so are we in the world. There is no fear in love, but perfect love casts out fear" (I John 4:17,18).

The other contrast which Paul intends to indicate is that between the people of God in the Old and New Testaments. This is not to infer, of course, that the faithful under the former covenant were altogether ignorant of the Spirit, but that He was not yet bestowed in abiding fulness. Nor was Christ revealed as the perfect fulfilment of the law and the only availing atonement for sin. So, in comparison with Gospel freedom, even the most devout were held under a certain measure of bondage (Gal. 4:1-3; cf. 3:23). It was the express design of Christ's advent that through Him believers might serve God "without fear" (Luke 1:74). And, as we gather from

Hebrews 2:14,15, "he himself . . . . partook of the same nature, that through death he might destroy him who has the power of death, that is, the devil, and deliver all those who through fear of death were subject to lifelong bondage."

So much, then, for the first part of this verse, with its miserable sequence of bondage, slavery and fear. The apostle tells his Roman readers that this is no longer their lot. "For you did *not* receive the spirit of slavery to fall back into fear, but you have received the spirit of sonship." Compare II Timothy 1:7 – "God did *not* give us a spirit of timidity but a spirit of power and love and self-control."

II. Next we are confronted by THE SPIRIT OF ADOPTION AND THE PRIVILEGE OF SONSHIP. This is the positive assertion of the verse. It tells us what Christians *have* received. We have received the spirit of adoption. It is a result of the Holy Spirit's penetration of our personality.

Adoption is one of the major terms of New Testament vocabulary. Literally it means "placing as a son" (*huiothesia*). It is common in classical Greek literature and on inscriptions to denote the legal adoption of sons, or sometimes daughters, though this was less frequent. In Scripture it is used metaphorically of God's relation to Israel, as in Romans 9:4. But in the four other cases where this word occurs, it has to do with the status of individual Christians. In Ephesians 1:5 we are told that God has predestinated us to the adoption of children through Jesus Christ, according to the purpose of His will. In Galatians 4:5 it is said that God's intention in sending forth His Son was "to redeem those who were under the law, so that we might receive adoption as sons." Here in Romans 8:15 we have the reference to the spirit of adoption and in v.23 we learn that believers enter into the full enjoyment of their adoption when the time of fulfilment releases them from the earthly body.

In order to understand Paul's meaning we must examine the details of adoption procedure in the Roman world. It was highly complicated and regarded as a serious step.

Dominating the whole conception of family life was the father's power – *patria potestas*. That power was absolute. It gave complete control. In Rome a son never came of age. No matter how old he was, he remained under the jurisdiction of his father. This was what made adoption so difficult. In the process a child had to pass from one *patria potestas* to another. He had to be removed from the oversight of one father and placed under the supervision of another. In Roman law this was an involved transaction.

There were two stages. The first was known as *mancipatio*, or freeing. The link with the natural father was dissolved in a symbolic sale in which he twice sold his son and twice bought him back. The third time he renounced his paternal rights and refrained from redeeming him: thus the father's power was held to be broken. The second step was called *vindicatio*. The adopting father applied to the magistrate and formally presented a petition in law for the transference of his prospective son to his *patria potestas*. Only when this long-drawn-out agreement had been signed and sealed was the adoption considered complete.

Dr. William Barclay, who explains all this most lucidly in his *Daily Study Bible*, lists four main consequences of adoption which light up what was in Paul's mind as he penned this verse. "(i) The adopted person lost all rights in his old family, and gained all the rights of a fully legitimate son in his new family. In the most literal sense, and in the most binding legal way, he got a new father. (ii) It followed that he became heir to his new father's estate. Even if other sons were afterwards born, who were real blood relations, it did not affect his rights. He was inalienably co-heir with them. (iii) In law, the old life of the adopted person was completely wiped out. For instance, legally all debts were cancelled; they were wiped out as if they had never been. The adopted person was regarded as a new person entering into a new life with which the past had nothing to do. (iv) In the eyes of the law the adopted person was literally and absolutely the son of his new father."

The length to which this went is strikingly illustrated in the case of the notorious Emperor Nero. He was adopted by his predecessor, Claudius. They were not even remotely related. In order to cement the alliance, Nero wished to marry Claudius's daughter Octavia. They were bound by no ties of blood. Yet in the sight of the law they were brother and sister and, before they could be united in wedlock, the Senate had to approve special legislation.

All this helps us to see what underlies the Scriptural teaching about adoption. As Sir William Ramsay put it, adoption was a kind of embryo will. It not only gave the adopted son all the privileges of real sonship, but it guaranteed the inheritance to him as well. Adoption, then, is the process by which we are accepted as sons of God, and this is effected as the Spirit engrafts us into the body of God's only-begotten Son, Jesus Christ. The consequence is that our spirit takes on a new tone. It is no longer servile: it reflects our recently acquired status and is thus rightly described as an adoption-spirit by contrast with the slave-spirit of sin and law.

Scripture thus preserves a clear distinction between children and sons. We are born again as children: we are adopted as sons. The one concerns our communion *with* God, and our partaking of the Divine nature: the other concerns our position *before* God, and our share of the Divine inheritance. These are complementary ideas, but the Word of God is careful to distinguish between them, although this is not always apparent in our Authorized Version and has to be corrected in more recent renderings. In John 1:12,13 we find that those who received Christ were given the right or authority "to become children of God" (not "sons" as A.V.) "who were born, not of blood nor of the will of the flesh nor of the will of man, but of God." Or again, in I John 3:1 – "See what love the Father has given us, that we should be called children of God (not "sons" as A.V.); and so we are." Now compare Luke 20:35,36 where an emendation is made in reverse, so to speak. "Those who are accounted worthy to attain to that age and to the resurrection from the dead neither marry nor are they given in marriage, for they cannot die any more, because they are equal to angels and are sons of God (not "children" as A.V.), being sons of the resurrection (not "children" as A.V.)." We are children of God, then, by virtue of regeneration; we are sons of God by virtue of adoption. "The two conceptions are evidently complementary," observed Bishop Westcott; "but they must be realized separately before the full force of the whole idea which they combine to give can be felt." In both instances the Holy Spirit plays a prominent part.

The spirit of bondage, then, with its entail of slavery and fear, is unfavourably matched with the spirit of adoption and the privilege of sonship, leading to the liberty which flows from trust.

III. This latter item must be highlighted as we find ourselves confronted by THE SPIRIT OF RECOGNITION AND THE ACKNOWLEDGEMENT OF FATHERHOOD. We assume that the exclamation, "Abba! Father!" does in fact belong to the sequence of this fifteenth verse and not to that which follows, as the Revised Standard Version implies by placing a full-stop after "the spirit of sonship." There is indeed an association of thought, but it is interesting to note that the New English Bible reverts to the more usual punctuation.

When a Christian has been born again and adopted into the family of God, a cry breaks from his lips. That is what is to be expected from a babe in Christ. When an infant is born, it cries. That is the sign of life. When we are born anew of the Spirit and enter into the inheritance of adoption prepared for the called of God, we shall emit a cry. And that cry will also be a word: the first word we frame as children and sons of God. There is great excitement in any household when baby utters his first word. Ears are strained to catch its import. It will no doubt be recorded in a family log-book. In nine cases out of ten,

if it is intelligible at all, and not simply a meaningless
gurgle, it is "Mummy" or "Daddy." So here we are told
that the first word the regenerate believer articulates is
"Father." Moreover, it is the Spirit who teaches us to
say it: this recognition is the response of the spirit within
us which has been recreated by the Holy Ghost and in-
structed by Him. It is the function of the Comforter to
impart the gift of spiritual speech. The Bible tells us that
no one can hail Jesus Christ as Lord except by the Holy
Spirit. It also tells us that no one can address God as
Father except by the Holy Spirit. The Spirit is the true
Introducer: He introduces us both to the Father and to
the Son. All this is confirmed in Galatians 4:6 – "And
because you are sons, God has sent the Spirit of his Son
into our hearts, crying, 'Abba! Father!'." This is the
Spirit's cry in us. He recognises God as Father through
our spirit.

"Abba" is simply the Aramaic form of father – and
Aramaic is the Palestinian dialect which our Lord Himself
spoke. When Jesus was praying in the garden of Gethsemane He approached His heavenly Father with this title
on His lips. "And going a little farther, he fell on the
ground and prayed that, if it were possible, the hour
might pass from him. And he said, 'Abba, Father, all
things are possible to thee; remove this cup from me;
yet not what I will, but what thou wilt' " (Mark 14:35,36).
In Aramaic the word was only used within the family
circle: it was an intimate name not employed by those
outside or even uttered in their presence. This was our
Lord's own personal name for His Father: it is really
"Abba, *the* Father," and the article has the force of a
possessive pronoun – "My own Father." There is, of
course, a unique relationship between the Divine Son
and the Divine Father which lends a profound significance
to that mode of address which it could never bear when
transferred to other lips. But, making allowance for that
distinction, it is nevertheless abundantly true that when
we become sons of God by adoption and grace, we share

the privilege of the real Son and can even dare to call God by His close family name. We can approach Him as did His only-begotten Son and this we would not dream of doing unless permitted and emboldened by the Holy Spirit.

These are the only instances in the New Testament where "Abba" occurs: in Mark's account of Gethsemane, and these parallel passages of Paul in Romans and Galatians relating to the adoption of the Spirit. "The Redeemer in His agony, the redeemed in their glory; sufferings and glory inter-related," says one commentator. "If we are soon to hear of sharing His sufferings, of joining in creation's groan, let us remember that we have the spirit of Christ, the spirit of sonship, whereby we cry, 'Abba, my Father'." Personal knowledge *of* the Father should evoke personal devotion *to* the Father.

> *My God! I know, I feel Thee mine,*
> *And will not quit my claim,*
> *Till all I have is lost in Thine*
> *And all renewed I am.*

What a contrast with the cry of the apostle in the previous chapter! Then the spirit of bondage caused him to exclaim, "Wretched man that I am! Who will deliver me from this body of death?" (Rom. 7:24). Now in the Spirit he joyfully recognizes the Divine graciousness and exultantly shouts "Abba! Father!"

How the Holy Spirit effects this recognition is indicated in Romans 5:5. He reveals to all believers the fatherly love of God as manifested in the atoning death of Christ. As Agar Beet memorably expressed it, "the Spirit speaks the Gospel to our hearts." We are brought to Calvary and shown the mystery of redeeming love. It is there that we learn not only that Christ is our Saviour but also that God is our Father. Charles Wesley portrays the wounds our Lord received on Calvary and rehearses the plea for pardon. Then he continues:

The Father hears Him pray,
His dear anointed One;
He cannot turn away
The presence of His Son:
His Spirit answers to the blood
And tells me I am born of God.

My God is reconciled,
His pardoning voice I hear;
He owns me for His child,
I can no longer fear;
With confidence I now draw nigh,
And Father, Abba Father! cry.

Matthew Cranswick, one of the pioneer missionaries in the West Indies, kept a record of more than two hundred people, young and old, who had received the most direct assurance of forgiveness and sonship while singing that great hymn of the eighteenth century Evangelical Awakening. When he had satisfied himself that a seeker was truly repentant, he would start to sing it, inviting the other to join in. "I have never known one instance," he testified, "of a sincere penitent failing to receive a joyous sense of pardon while singing that hymn." The reason was, of course, that it is entirely Scriptural and although more recently some have sniffed at its theology as being outmoded and unsuitable to the modern age, it none-the-less enshrines the eternal truth of God concerning the relationship between the shedding of Christ's blood and the adoption of the Spirit. The price that was paid in order that we might become the sons of God was the unblemished sacrifice of Calvary. While we rejoice in the experience, let us never forget the infinite cost.

Nor must we overlook the priority of the Father's will in the whole procedure of adoption. It is not our recognition of God but His recognition of us which constitutes the core of this conception. In that sense our adoption precedes our regeneration. His decision to make us sons lies behind the act which begets us as His children. The transaction which transfers the believer to his new *patria potestas* in God took place at the Cross. We have enjoyed the status of sons in the eternal purposes of God since before the world began, and at Calvary He devised the means whereby it could be conveyed to us. In regeneration, that change is wrought in our nature which recreates us as children of God so that we become inwardly what by adoption He has made us outwardly. And yet the awareness of such adoption can be awakened in us only after we have been born again. It is then that the Holy Spirit touches our spirit and testifies first that we are sons (Rom. 8:15) and then children of God (v.16).

"Could anything disclose the marvel of adoption," asks John Murray, "or certify the security of its tenure and privilege more effectively than the fact that the Father himself, on account of whom are all things and through whom are all things, who made the Captain of salvation perfect through sufferings, becomes by deed of grace the Father of the many sons whom He will bring to glory? And that is the reason why the Captain of salvation Himself is not ashamed to call them brethren and can exult with joy unspeakable, 'Behold I and the children whom God hath given to me' (Heb. 2:13)." This attitude of adoring wonderment at what God has in grace and mercy elected to achieve by naming us as His sons must ensure that we close this study of v.15 in the spirit of prayer and praise.

CHAPTER SEVEN

THE WITNESS OF THE SPIRIT

ALTHOUGH FOR THE PURPOSES of convenient exposition
we are looking separately at each passage in Romans
Eight dealing with the Holy Spirit, the whole chapter,
of course, hangs together and one section moves smoothly
into the next. That is so in relation to verses 14, 15 and
16. Verse 14 deals with the guidance of the Spirit, but in
speaking about the sons of God it leads naturally to verse
15 which refers to the adoption of the Spirit. This in turn
merges unobtrusively into verse 16 which alludes to the
witness of the Spirit and really returns to verse 14, for the
effect of the Spirit's testimony is to confirm our filial
relationship with our heavenly Father. Whilst, therefore,
we examine these three verses one after another, we must
recognize that they are really all of a piece.

Commenting on verse 15, Martin Luther wrote: "Such
is the description of the Kingdom of Christ: such is the
veritable work and the notable service of God: such is
the operation of the Spirit in the believer." Now in verse 16
the apostle proceeds to deal with the Spirit's own confirmation of the Christian's adoption into the Divine
family. T. H. Green, the distinguished Oxford philosopher,
once declared that the greatest verses in the Bible were
the 16th and 26th of Romans Eight. Most certainly they
are amongst the red-letter texts and we should do well
to mark them.

There could be no better introduction to this vital
verse than John Wesley's classic definition of the Spirit's
witness in one of his Standard Sermons. With an obvious
echo of his own experience in Aldersgate Street he declares

88

that it is "an inward impression on the soul, whereby the Spirit of God directly witnesses to my spirit, that I am a child of God; that Jesus Christ hath loved me, and given Himself for me; and that all my sins are blotted out, and I, even I, am reconciled to God."

We must begin by elucidating another link between verse 16 and its predecessor. What Paul says here is still in the setting of Roman legal procedure with relation to adoption. The actual ceremony whereby a person was transferred to another family had to be carried out in the presence of no less than seven witnesses. The function of these witnesses was not fulfilled when they had seen the transaction completed. They might be called upon later to uphold the claim of the adopted man to be regarded as a son. If the adopting father died and there was a dispute about the disposal of the property, then one of the witnesses might well be summoned. "I was present at the ceremony," he would swear. "It was I who held the scales and struck them with the ingot of brass. It was a genuine adoption. I heard the words of the vindication, and I testify that this person was claimed by the deceased, not as a slave, but as a son." So, by the word of the witness, the right of the adopted person was guaranteed and he entered into his inheritance. Now what Paul is saying here is this: that the Holy Spirit Himself is the witness to the believer's adoption into the family of God.

I. We shall touch upon four aspects of the Spirit's witness, in order to bring out its fullest significance. The first is THE BEARER OF THE WITNESS. It is, of course, none other than the Holy Spirit who acts as witness. "It is the Spirit himself." Right away we must clear up the difficulty created by the Authorized Version rendering "itself." That has puzzled many simple believers who have been rightly taught that the Holy Ghost is a person not a thing. Sometimes those who ought to know better fall, perhaps unthinkingly, into the heretical trap of speaking about "it" instead of "Him." And, of course, there are others who have reduced the Christian doctrine of the Spirit beyond all recognition and for whom the Spirit is indeed no more than an impersonal influence, properly designated as "it."

But we have not so learned Christ, nor have we so read God's Word. The opening pages of René Pache's masterly study of *The Person and Work of the Holy Spirit* set out the Scriptural evidence in quite unmistakeable fashion. His summary is worth reproducing, for it supplies much-needed material when defending the faith against those who deny the truth of the Trinity.

I. THE HOLY SPIRIT ACTS AS A PERSON. Let us note some of the actions which are attributed to Him and cannot be the expression of a power or of a thing. 1. *He dwells* in believers (John 14:17). 2. *He teaches;* He brings to remembrance (John 14:26). 3. *He testifies* (John 15:26). 4. *He convicts* of sin (John 16:8). 5. *He guides* into all truth; He hears, He speaks, He shows (John 16:13). 6. *He inspires* Scripture and speaks through it (Acts 1:16; II Pet. 1:21). 7. *He spoke* to Philip (Acts 8:29). 8. *He calls* to the ministry (Acts 13:2). 9. *He sends forth* His servants (Acts 13:4). 10. *He forbids* certain actions (Acts 16:6,7). 11. *He intercedes,* etc. (Rom. 8:26).

II. HE POSSESSES THE ESSENTIAL ATTRIBUTES OF PERSONALITY. The Spirit is endued with 1. *A will:* He bestows His gifts upon every man as He will. 2. *Thought:* God knows what is the mind of the Spirit (Rom. 8:27). 3. *Knowledge:* The Spirit knows and searches the things of God (I Cor. 2:10,11). 4. *Language:* "We speak, not in words which man's wisdom teacheth, but which the Spirit teacheth, comparing spiritual things with spiritual" (I Cor. 2:13). 5. *Love:* Paul exhorts the Romans for the love of the Spirit to strive together with him in their prayers (Rom. 15:30). 6. *Goodness:* "Thou gavest . . . . Thy good Spirit to instruct them" (Neh. 9:20).

III. THE NAMES WHICH ARE GIVEN HIM REVEAL BOTH HIS PERSONALITY AND HIS DIVINITY. 1. He is called: (a). My Spirit (Gen. 6:3). (b). The Spirit of God (II Chron. 15:1).

(c). The Spirit of the Lord (Isa. 11:2). (d). The breath of the Almighty (Job 32:8). (e). The Spirit of the Lord God (Isa. 61:1). (f). The Spirit of your Father (Matt. 10:20). (g). The Spirit of Jesus (Acts 16:7). (h). The Spirit of Christ (Rom. 8:9). (i). The Spirit of His Son (Gal. 4:6). Since the three divine Persons are one, it is not surprising that the Holy Spirit should receive without distinction one or the other of these appellations. 2. His other names completely demonstrate His qualities. He is the Spirit: (a). Of holiness – the Holy Spirit (Psa. 51:11; Rom. 1:4). (b). Of wisdom (Isa. 11:2). (c). Of counsel (Isa. 11:2). (d). Of understanding (Isa. 11:2). (e). Of supplications (Zech. 12:10). (f). Of worship (John 4:23). (g). Of truth (John 14:17). (h). Of comfort (John 14:26 – the Comforter). (i). Of life (Rom. 8:2). (j). Of adoption (Rom. 8:15). (k). Of faith (II Cor. 4:13). (l) Of love (II Tim. 1:7). (m). Of might (II Tim. 1:7). (n). Of sound judgment (II Tim. 1:7, Weymouth). (o). Of revelation (Eph. 1:17). (p). Of power (Eph. 3:20; Rom. 15:13 – the power of the Holy Ghost). (q). Of eternity – the eternal Spirit (Heb. 9:14). (r). Of grace (Heb. 10:29). (s). Of glory (I Pet. 4:14).

IV. THE SPIRIT CAN BE TREATED LIKE A PERSON. He can be: 1. *Lied to* (Acts 5:3). 2. *Tempted* (Acts 5:9). 3. *Resisted* (Acts 7:51). 4. *Grieved* (Eph. 4:30). 5. *Outraged* (Heb. 10:29). 6. *Blasphemed against* (Matt. 12:21). 7. *Called upon* (Ezek. 37:9).

There is one further item of evidence mentioned by Dr. Pache which we shall introduce shortly, namely that of our Lord's own use of a personal pronoun when speaking of the Spirit, but sufficient has been quoted to meet every possible objection and resolve each genuine doubt. "The witness of the New Testament is clear enough," concludes Dr. Leon Morris (and what he says can include the Old Testament testimony so far as it goes). "The Spirit is thought of consistently as a Person, and as a Person in some sense distinct from though closely related to, the Father and the Son. Nor is He another name for one aspect of the Father or the Son. He is a Person in His own right, with His own functions."

This being so, how does it come about that in the Authorized Version rendering of Romans 8:16 we read of the Spirit "itself?" The explanation is really quite simple. We must remember that whilst the English language has discarded the use of grammatical gender, others have retained it. In our tongue everything is delightfully simple. Sex is determinative. Males are denoted by the masculine and females by the feminine. The remainder are bound to be neuter, even though we may habitually refer to a ship as "she." Now English stands alone in this respect amongst the major languages, either ancient or modern. With us the word 'pen' is neuter. In French it is feminine – *la plume*. But, of course, it would not be a correct translation into English to make a pen female and call it "she." In other words, grammatical gender bears no relation to male or female, personal or impersonal, when we are dealing with a language other than English. The Greek word for head (*kephalē*) is feminine, but that does not prevent the Scripture from speaking about Christ as the Head of His Body the Church.

The word for Spirit (*pneuma*) is neuter in Greek and so, in accordance with the rules of construction, is followed by the neuter pronoun "it," just as *kephalē* would be followed by the feminine pronoun "she." But this is purely a grammatical form. It has no theological significance whatsoever. In no way does it bear upon the nature of the Holy Spirit or for one moment suggest impersonality. The Authorized Version is being very strictly literal and we may feel more than a little pedantic in insisting upon "itself." What we have to do is to apply all that we learn elsewhere from Scripture about the personality of the Holy Spirit: if we do this, then we shall follow the Revised Version, the Revised Standard Version and most recent translations and render "Himself" instead. The New English Bible, incidentally, neatly circumvents the problem by translating: "in that cry the Spirit of God joins

with our spirit in testifying that we are God's children."
But there is no need to take evasive action like that.

Here in Romans 8:16 strict grammatical rectitude is
observed. The apostle Paul did not feel at liberty to play
about with the rules of language in order to put his meaning
altogether beyond doubt. But it is significant that when
our Lord referred to the Holy Spirit (and here we pick
up the last item of evidence listed by Dr. Pache as sub-
stantiating His personality), He deliberately set aside the
canons of construction, as He had the authority to do, and
allowed a masculine pronoun to follow the neuter substantive *pneuma* (John 14:26; 16:7,8,13,14). "He" in 14:26;
16:8,13 and 14 is emphatically personal – "He Himself."

Nevertheless, despite the irrefutable testimony both of
Scripture and our Lord's own authoritative teaching and
usage as recorded in Scripture, many people – even
Christian people – still find it hard to think of the Holy
Spirit in terms of personality. This is largely due, no doubt,
to what we may describe with all reverence as the humility
of the Holy Spirit. He never attracts attention to Himself.
His office is to glorify Christ. He is best seen in His effect
on lives transformed by His touch into the likeness of
our Lord. "We most easily recognize the Spirit," wrote
Evelyn Underhill, "when it (*sic*) is perceived transfiguring
human character."

For those who are at all troubled because they cannot
precisely identify the Holy Spirit in their experience in
distinction from the Father and the Son, a story about
Dr. Griffith Thomas will convey a message of encourage-
ment. He once received a letter from a woman in which
she confessed: "I have prayed, I have read the Bible,
I have striven. I have done all that I can and still I am
not sure whether I have the fulness of the Spirit." And
this was the wise advice of that great evangelical theologian:
"Turn your thought out, not in. What is Christ to you?
If He is little, you have not the fulness of the Spirit. If
He is chief among ten thousand and altogether lovely,
you have the fulness of the Spirit."

The verb in this 16th verse must next concern us. It is translated "bearing witness with." The noun "witness" is *martus*, from which comes martyr. That was what it cost to be a witness in New Testament times – and the price is demanded today where the fight is fiercest. To bear witness, or testify, is *martureō*. Here the prefix *sun* (with) is supplied and the resultant verb is *summartureō*, which means to confirm or testify in support of someone or something. The suggestion is that the Holy Spirit is a joint- or co-witness. As we saw in the previous verse, the Spirit of adoption enables us to cry "Abba! Father!" and that recognition of our own spirit is not only prompted but also corroborated by the Holy Spirit.

The varied witness of the Spirit is often mentioned in the New Testament. Let us look at some of the occurrences. In Acts 15:8 Peter declares concerning the Gentiles that "God who knows the heart bore witness to them, giving them the Holy Spirit just as he did to us" (*cf.* Acts 10:44,47; 11:15). In Hebrews 10:15 the Holy Spirit is described as a witness to the new covenant in the blood of Christ. In I John 5:7 we read: "And the Spirit is the witness, because the Spirit is truth." Two other verses in the First Epistle of John speak quite explicitly of this specific witness of the Spirit to the believer's sonship. "All who keep his commandments abide in him, and he in them. And by this we know that he abides in us, by the Spirit which he has given us" (I John 3:24). The same difficulty with the neuter, "which," arises here. N.E.B. again gets round it: "we know it from the Spirit he has given us." But we could legitimately put "whom" as does the Amplified New Testament. "By this we know that we abide in him and he in us, because he has given us of his own Spirit" (I John 4:13). These twin texts from John will serve to clinch the identity of the witness.

II. We must deal more briefly with THE NATURE OF THE WITNESS. The Holy Spirit bears testimony in conjunction with our own spirit. In other words, it is an inward witness. This *testimonium internum Spiritus Sancti*, as the Reformers designated it, is a fundamental feature of our Protestant and evangelical message. It is primarily a witness which confirms what is already assured to the believer by the Word of God. It is on the authority of Scripture that we recognize ourselves as God's children and the Holy Spirit, who Himself inspired the written Word, comes to provide an inner confirmation of the outward revelation. Said Calvin: "Just as God alone is a fitting witness concerning Himself in His utterance, so also the utterance will not find faith in the hearts of men before it is sealed by the inner witness of the Spirit. The same Spirit, therefore, who spoke by the mouth of the prophets, must of necessity penetrate our hearts to persuade us that what was divinely commanded has been faithfully published." And again: "The Word itself is not fully certain to us unless it is confirmed by the witness of the Spirit. God sent the same Spirit, by whose virtue He had administered the Word, to complete His own work by the effective confirmation of the Word."

The distinction between the Divine Spirit and the human spirit is nowhere clearer than in this verse and yet at the same time their close relationship is equally apparent. The Spirit of God and the spirit of redeemed and regenerated man collaborate in this mutual testimony. As Phillips has it, "the Spirit Himself endorses our inward conviction that we really are the children of God." The spirit is that in man to which God can speak and appeal. That is why Proverbs 20:27 can tell us that "the spirit of man is the lamp of the Lord." It can be lit at His flame and burn for His glory. The witness of our own spirit is almost identical with "the testimony of our conscience" to which Paul refers in I Corinthians 1:12. On the only occasions when this verb *summartureō* appears in the New Testament apart from this verse, it is linked with conscience. Both instances are in Romans. In 2:15 Paul says (concerning Gentiles who are without the law and yet do by nature what the law requires): "They show that what the law requires is written on their hearts, while their conscience also bears witness." In 9:1 he declares: "I am speaking the truth in Christ, I am not lying; my conscience bears me witness in the Holy Ghost, that I have great sorrow and unceasing anguish in my heart." "God the Holy Ghost does not in His testimony supersede conscience," Dr. W. B. Pope insisted: "He honours that ancient representative of the Divine voice within the nature of man; and never disjoins His evidence from that of the subjective moral consciousness which condemns or approves – in this case approves – according to the standard of law written on the heart, or the conscience objective. He is indeed 'greater than our heart' – or conscience – 'and knoweth all things'. He knoweth the mystery of the Atonement and may silence the condemning heart. But if He assures of pardon He commits the assurance to the conscience as its guardian; so that 'if our heart condemn us not, then have we confidence towards God'."

The witness of the Spirit, then, is no fantastic demonstration. It is not a spectacular outward manifestation, but a calm, unobtrusive inward assurance. "Ecstasies and illuminations, inspirations and intuitions, are not necessary," asserts Karl Barth. "Happy are they who are worthy to receive them! But, woe be to us if we anxiously wait for them! Woe be to us, if we fail to recognize that they are patchwork by-products. All that occurs *to* us and *in* us can be no more than an answer to what the Spirit Himself says." The emphasis, then, is on inwardness. The Holy Spirit is no exhibitionist. "He who believes in the Son of God has the testimony in himself" (I John5: 10).

It is perfectly evident from Scripture, of course, that the witness of our spirit is no more than a response to the witness of God's Spirit. "That this testimony must needs in the very nature of things be antecedent to the testimony of our own spirit," argued John Wesley, "may appear from this single consideration. We must be holy of heart and holy in life before we can be conscious that we are so;

before we can have the testimony of our spirit that we are inwardly and outwardly holy. But we must love God, before we can be holy at all; this being the root of all holiness. Now we cannot love God till we know that He loves us. And we cannot know His pardoning love to us till His Spirit witnesses it to our spirit. Since, therefore, the testimony of His Spirit must precede the love of God and all holiness, of consequence it must precede our consciousness thereof, or the testimony of our spirit concerning them."

To produce a perfect chord of music two notes are necessary. They must be attuned to each other. Unless there is such adjustment when they are struck, instead of the faultless chord there will be jarring dissonance. So the witness of God's Spirit with our spirit can only be perfectly harmonious when our wills are aligned with His. Then it is indeed a joint witness, according to its nature as described in this verse.

III. We must discuss THE CONTENT OF THE WITNESS. The Holy Spirit creates in believers a sense of their filial relationship to their Father in heaven. He bears testimony that we are in fact the children of God. And that is a staggering confirmation to be sure. "We – God's children!" exclaims Barth. "Consider and bear in mind the vast unobservability, impossibility and paradox of these words. Remember that, in daring this predication, we are taking the miraculous, primal, creative step which Abraham took; we are taking the step of faith, the step over the abyss from the old to the new creation, which God alone can take. We – God's children! In uttering these words either we are talking blasphemy or we are singing the song of the redeemed."

Although this astonishing disclosure is an inward impression upon the soul, it is nevertheless conveyed by an external power. It is as important to stress the objective nature of the Spirit's testimony as it is to recognize its inner application. Ultimately this is the only safeguard we possess against an experience which is purely subjective. It is the constant charge of our critics that our testimony as Christians is something we have produced from within ourselves. It carries little weight with the thinking unbeliever because he seeks to explain it all away as self-induced. He wants some evidence beyond ourselves. The doctrine and experience of the Spirit's witness confirms the fact that the phenomena of Christian faith are not self-originated, as Dr. Maldwyn Hughes expressed it, but brought into being by the power of God. "Our consciousness of the forgiveness of sins," he continued, "of our filial relation to God and our fellowship with Him, of the new life which He brings to birth within us, of the grace which He gives us in times of temptation and of the comfort wherewith He blesses us in days of sorrow – these are not the product of our own imagination and feeling, but are the fruits of the literal indwelling of Christ within us."

What the Spirit witnesses, then, in conjunction with our spirit, is our sonship by adoption and our new birth as the children of God. And in verse 17 Paul glimpses some of the implications of our relationship to God. The clue here lies in the little preposition "with." It is prefixed to three words. The first is a noun and the other two are verbs. "And if children, then heirs, heirs of God and fellow-heirs with Christ" – literally, "with-heirs of Christ." We are God's own inheritors jointly with our Lord. But, lest that glorious prospect should so dazzle us that we fail to realize the path that leads to it, we are reminded that Christ's way led by a cross to the heavenly throne. That must be our road too. "Provided we suffer with him in order that we may also be glorified with him."

We have to "with-suffer" if we are to be "with-glorified." "Sufferings are intrinsic to the Gospel," urges Elton Trueblood, "and every Christian must be personally involved in them."

The sufferings of Christ are to be looked at from two points of view. On the one hand, He suffered as the propitiation for our sins. On the other hand, His sufferings were the vestibule to glory. In the first, of course, we have no share. Christ alone has suffered for sin: Christ alone made satisfaction to the justice of God: Christ alone purchased eternal redemption. His suffering to make atonement for man's sin was unique and unrepeatable. He was "offered once to bear the sins of many" (Heb. 9:28; cf.10:10 "once for all"). But insofar as our Lord's sufferings paved the pathway to glory, He has left an example that we should follow in His steps. The Calvary road is one we all must take. There is no escape. "Indeed all who desire to live a godly life in Christ Jesus will be persecuted" (II Tim. 3:12). But the end is glory. After the cross, the crown. It is for the joy that is set before us that, with our blessed Lord, we can endure the cross and despise the shame. The same association of suffering and glory is found again in verse 18 where we shall be dealing with it at greater length.

This firm anchorage of the Spirit's witness in the hard facts of Christian life guards it from sentimental or superficial misunderstanding. Blessed assurance is something more than a warm feeling inside that makes us sing out with zest when the popular chorus is announced. It should make us want to sing, but its basis is more secure and permanent than our vacillating emotions. It rests upon what God has done for us in Christ and it is none other than the Spirit Himself who seals it to us. And it is always confirmed in a life that is in line with that of Christ Himself. Unless we are taking His way, we cannot be His brethren. It is of the essence of discipleship that we should be with our Lord. That is why He called the twelve. That is why He calls us. We are to be with Him in suffering that afterwards we may be with Him in glory. Let no one pretend to the witness of the Spirit who is not treading in the Master's steps. "A spiritual conviction, however deep and assuring," M. R. Terry reminds us, "needs the constant test of verification in a pure and upright life."

IV. In closing our study of these two verses we must define THE OCCASION OF THE WITNESS. This need not occupy us long. The ringing answer of God's Word is *now*. Assurance is not a deferred benefit. We do not have to wait until we arrive in heaven to enjoy it. It is not even postponed until we have reached some special height of holiness. It is a present experience. It can be ours at this very moment. We can know that we are children of God and we can know now.

The New Testament quite unambiguously alludes to those who have actually entered into such an assurance. Paul reminds the Ephesians that "in him you also, who have heard the word of truth, the gospel of your salvation, and have believed in him, were sealed with the promised Holy Spirit, which is the guarantee of our inheritance until we acquire possession of it, to the praise of his glory" (Eph. 1:13,14). It is the first instalment, presaging even better things in store, but it is available now. Neither the seal nor the earnest of the Spirit are thought of as future: what they betoken lies ahead, but the assurance they bring is present (*cf.* Eph. 4:30 – "Do not grieve the Holy Spirit of God, in whom you were sealed for the day of redemption" II Corinthians 1:21,22 – "But it is God who establishes us with you in Christ, and has commissioned us; he has put his seal upon us and given us his Spirit in our hearts as a guarantee").

This being so, whilst we must be careful not to elevate a conscious and articulate assurance into a test of salvation (for, according to the Westminster Confession, it "doth not so belong to the essence of faith, but that a true believer may wait long, and conflict with many difficulties, before he be a partaker of it"), it is nevertheless a Scriptural injunction that we should be zealous to confirm our call and election, for if we do this we will never fall (II Pet. 1:10). Hence, should we not yet enjoy this privilege, we are entitled to expect it and indeed encouraged to seek it. Some fervent, pleading words of Octavius Winslow, must press home to the reader the implications of this searching couplet from Romans Eight: "To the child of God we would say, covet earnestly the witness of the Spirit. Do not be cast down, nor cherish rash and hasty conclusions as to your adoption, if you do not possess it so fully and clearly as others. The holiest believer may walk for many days without the sun. Read the record of the experiences of David and of Job and of Jeremiah, and of the last moments of our dear and adorable Immanuel, and mark what shadows at times fell upon their souls, how a sense of comfort failed them, how joys fled, and they mourned an absent God. But were they the less dear to the heart of Jehovah? Were they less His beloved children because they were thus tried? No! God forbid! Still, we plead for the full enjoyment of the witness of the Spirit. It is the high privilege of the children of God – let no one rob them of it – to look up to God, and humbly yet unceasingly cry, 'Abba, Father!'."

CHAPTER EIGHT

THE FIRST FRUITS OF THE SPIRIT

THERE WERE THREE MAJOR FEASTS in the Old Testament dispensation, when the Jews were required to appear before God in the holy temple at Jerusalem. There was the Passover, which commemorated the exodus from Egypt and was symbolized by the eating of unleavened bread and the offering of the paschal lamb. There was the Feast of Tabernacles or Booths, which commemorated Israel's wanderings in the wilderness and eventual entrance into the land of promise, symbolized by the erection of tents and the waving of triumphal tree-branches.

Between these two celebrations in the Jewish year lay the Feast of Weeks, or Pentecost. It was so designated because it was observed on the fiftieth day following the Passover sabbath. In Leviticus 23:15-17 the words of institution are recorded. "And you shall count from the morrow after the sabbath, from the day that you brought the sheaf of the wave offering; seven full weeks shall they be, counting fifty days to the morrow after the seventh sabbath; then you shall present a cereal offering of new grain to the Lord. You shall bring from your dwellings two loaves of bread to be waved, made of two-tenths of an ephah; they shall be of fine flour, they shall be baked with leaven, as first fruits to the Lord." In the book of Exodus it is more briefly described: "And you shall observe the feast of weeks, the first fruits of wheat harvest, and the feast of ingathering at the year's end" (Exod. 34:22). The Feast of Weeks is there associated, of course, with the Feast of Tabernacles, the one being celebrated at the beginning and the other at the end of the harvest.

102

Over many centuries Israel was an agricultural nation, relying for her sustenance on the produce of the land. Pentecost was the festival which marked the presentation of the first fruits of the wheat harvest, when Israel expressed her dependence upon God for daily bread. Like our Whitsuntide, the Feast of Weeks was a popular holiday. It fell in early summer when the skies of the Holy Land were innocent of clouds, the weather encouragingly warm and as yet unspoilt by the scorching desert wind, the Hamsin. From every part of the country the faithful would stream into Jerusalem to appear before their God. Many visitors from abroad amongst the Jews of the Dispersion would also make for the Holy City. The feast of the first fruits was a high festival.

Now it is of exceptional significance for us as Christians that the initial outpouring of the Spirit's fulness occurred on the Day of Pentecost. Indeed, it was with the bestowal of the Comforter that this celebration of the former dispensation reached its fulfilment. As Victor Buksbazen brings out in his informative book, *The Gospel in the Feasts of Israel*, from which much of the foregoing material has been drawn, it is a feature of these festivals that each foreshadows some event in the drama of redemption recorded in the Scriptures of the New Testament which discloses the substance of what they dimly symbolized. This is nowhere more apparent than in the case of Pentecost. The mighty, miraculous occurrences of Acts Two reveal what all along this annual feast had been forecasting. Indeed, the day was kept in the richness of its significance for the first time only when the Holy Ghost was given. Incidentally, that is why the translation of Acts 2:1 in the New English Bible is so inadequate "While the day of Pentecost was running its course" – that is a trite and mundane introduction to the epic event, suggesting that Pentecost was on a par with any other day. But the intention of the original text is much deeper than that. The Authorized Version has captured the sense of consummation – "When the day of Pentecost was fully come." The word means "to fill up completely." It is used in Luke 8:23 to describe how, during the storm on the lake, the boat in which Jesus and the disciples were sailing began to fill up with water so that it was in danger of sinking. The only other time the verb appears in the New Testament is also in Luke, and, most significantly, has to do with the fulfilment of prophecy. "When the days *drew near* for him to be received up, he set his face to go to Jerusalem" (Luke 9:51). This is the preface to the passion narrative, in which our Lord was to complete the meaning of the Passover Feast by Himself becoming the Paschal Lamb sacrified for the sins of the world. This verse in Acts 2:1 similarly paves the way for another fulfilment, namely, that of the Feast of Weeks in the bestowal of the first fruits of the Spirit. It was in this sense that the day of Pentecost had fully come – it never had fully come before. Only now was its meaning made plain. What had for centuries been indirectly set forth in Jewish observance became a vivid reality. The type was superseded: the Comforter Himself was come.

We cannot escape the coincidence involved in the giving of the Spirit at the feast of the first fruits. There is a most instructive congruity about it. In this meaningful association we are taught a vital truth concerning the Holy Spirit. He Himself is a kind of first fruits. For the phrase "the first fruits of the Spirit" is not intended to imply that He is in any way divided and that what we enjoy now is only some part of His fulness. The genitive is in apposition: the first fruits *are* the Spirit. He is a fore-taste of future glory. God gives Him to the believer as an anticipation of heaven. That is the revelation contained in the central verse in the section from Romans 8:18–25 which lies before us at the moment. We shall be expounding the whole passage, but we must ring round verse 23 as the key text. "We ourselves, who have the first fruits of the Spirit" – that is the aspect of the Pentecostal gift with which we are next concerned.

The immediate link in the preceding paragraph is

with verse 15, where Paul talks about the Spirit of adoption. But he realizes that such adoption is incomplete. It is assured to the believer, but it is not yet apparent to the world. It is a concealed sonship. It is obscured by the body of our humiliation. But at the end of the age, when the Lord returns for His own and then with His own, that sonship will be revealed. All will see that adoption is a fact. The Spirit is the first fruits of that coming disclosure. "Beloved, we are God's children now; it does not yet appear what we shall be, but we know that when he appears we shall be like him, for we shall see him as he is" (I John 3:2).

There are two words used by Paul in his epistles to convey this truth. Writing to Corinth, with its mercantile interests, he alludes to the earnest or guarantee of the Spirit (II Cor. 1:22; 5:5). *Arrabōn* really means part-payment on an assignment of goods, the first instalment which pledges the delivery of the rest. It is also applied in modern Greek to an engagement ring, where the same idea is romantically present. The Holy Spirit, then, is our earnest of good things to come.

But writing to Rome, with its considerable Jewish colony, Paul is led to utilize another metaphor – this of the *aparchē* or first fruit, with its reference to the feast of Israel. The Holy Spirit represents the specimen crop of glory yet to be. The grapes of Eschol, brought back by Caleb and Joshua after their reconnoitre of the Promised Land, were meant to whet the appetite for the eventual entry. So the Holy Spirit adds incentive to the life of holiness by introducing us to a taste of heaven on earth. The Christian enjoys heaven below as well as heaven above. He makes the best of both worlds.

> *The men of grace have found*
> *Glory begun below;*
> *Celestial fruit on earthly ground*
> *From faith and hope may grow.*

The section from v.18–25 in Romans Eight may be

subdivided into four parts, each with two contrasted keywords.

I. SUFFERING AND GLORY (vv.18,19). The apostle picks up the theme of the previous verse, where he has said that if we share Christ's sufferings now we shall share His glory hereafter. But if we are to endure such suffering we shall need the strength that only the Comforter can provide. "Therefore the Holy Spirit must be our schoolmaster," said Luther, "and send comfort into our hearts."

"For," Paul goes on in v.18 (A.V.) – that is, in order that we may the better grasp what has just been said about our identification with Christ's sufferings and His glory – "I reckon." That is more than the "I consider" of the Revised Standard Version or Moffatt's "I hold." It means to assess, to calculate, to count up the pros and cons. Paul has done some mental arithmetic. He has made a swift estimate. He has set out a profit and loss account. And on the basis of personal experience, for he speaks of what he knows, he declares that the balance falls in favour of glory. The sufferings are merely temporary: the glory is everlasting. He comes to the same conclusion in II Corinthians 4:17,18: "For this slight momentary affliction is preparing for us an eternal weight of glory beyond all comparison, because we look not to the things that are seen but to the things that are unseen; for the things that are seen are transient, but the things that are unseen are eternal." Bernard of Clairvaux amplified this: "The sufferings of this time are not worthy to be compared to the past sins remitted, the present grace of consolation, the future glory which is promised." And Luther seized upon the contrast: "See how he contracts the suffering of the world into a single drop and a tiny spark, whilst he expands its glory into a mighty ocean and a blaze of fire."

Suffering belongs to "this present time." The Greek really is "the now time," which accords with "until now" in verse 22. The Scripture is most exact in its chronology.

Everything is carefully allotted to its appropriate dispensation. Suffering belongs to "the now time" between the advents of our Lord. Glory belongs to "the then time" at the end of this age. And the one bears no kind of comparison with the other: as Moffatt has it, the suffering is "a mere nothing" when set against the coming glory.

In James 2:1 our Lord Jesus Christ is referred to as "the glory." Most English translations fail to convey that fact, although the italics in the Authorized Version hint at its presence. But in his interlinear New Testament, Dr. Alfred Marshall quite rightly sets "the glory" in apposition to "our Lord Jesus Christ," and cites Luke 2:32 where in Simeon's *Nunc Dimittis*, Christ is similarly described as the glory of God's people Israel. He is the true Shekinah. It may well have been that the manifestations of the Divine glory recorded in the Old Testament were, in fact, expressed through the second Person of the Holy Trinity. Certainly at the Baptism and even more obviously at the Transfiguration, our Lord shone in Shekinah glory. And at the end, He will return not only *in* glory, but *as* glory. Christ Himself is "the glory Who shall be revealed" (the Greek is capable of such an interpretation) at the close of the age bounded by "now." "Shall be" is emphatic: He is destined so to be manifest in the unchangeable purpose of God.

All this, we are told, is with us in view. The Revised Version has "to usward;" the Revised Standard Version "to us" and the New English Bible "in store for us." But whilst the little preposition employed here can carry all these possibilities, there are experts who feel that the Authorized Version was nearest to the mark with "in." The Amplified New Testament puts them all together and has "the glory that is about to be revealed to us and in us and for us and conferred upon us." This is a glory which will not only engross our vision but transform our whole being. It is like the magic mirror in the fairy tale which changes the appearance of those who gaze into it.

When our eyes behold Him Who is the glory, we shall be transfigured into His own image. As we learned from v.17, we shall be glorified with Him.

According to the late Professor G. T. Thomson of Edinburgh, in v.19 Paul "states a scientific fact viewed theologically." The entire natural world is waiting for that consummation devoutly to be desired. This manifestation, or apocalypse, of the sons of God is "the one far-off divine event to which the whole creation moves." "Eager longing" is a most expressive term. It indicates a straining forward, like crowds at a stadium as the competitors speed past. Literally, it is "watching with outstretched head." It is a picture of a man craning his neck to catch sight of what is approaching. This is further strengthened by the verb "waits" which suggests concentrated endurance, hanging on in patience until what is expected happens. Phillips is most apt: "The whole creation is on tiptoe to see the wonderful sight of the sons of God coming into their own."

All this is said, not of human beings, but of animate and inanimate nature as distinct from mankind. It does not apply to the children of God, for they are expressly distinguished in this very verse. It does not apply to the unregenerate, for they entertain no such expectation. "The creation" here means the natural order, cursed as it is in consequence of Adam's fall.

II. BONDAGE AND DELIVERANCE (vv.20,21). The creation, mentioned in v.19, we are now told was put under subjection by God's decree after the fall. "It was made the victim of frustration" (N.E.B.). "Vanity" in the Authorized Version is really meaninglessness, lack of purpose, dissatisfaction. It is a word which relates to that which fails to reach its end. Dake has "disappointing misery." The Gentiles walk, Paul tells the Ephesians, "in the *futility* of their minds" (Eph. 4:17). Those who have forsaken the right way, says Peter, utter "loud boasts of *folly*" (II Pet. 2:18). The word is the same in each case. What could more trenchantly epitomize the modern mood? It would seem that this sense of purposelessness and malaise which characterizes the natural world since the entry of sin, has transferred itself also to the natural man. Indeed, as this verse reminds us, the process is actually in reverse, for it is because of man's transgression that nature has been blighted. Nature and man share the same bondage. And the space age, with all the marvels that science places at our elbow, brings no relief from this fundamental dispeace. There is abroad today a sinister spirit of nihilism. "*Nichavo* – nothing matters" is the fashionable motto. "Let us eat, drink and be merry," decide our contemporary Epicureans, "for in the nuclear tomorrow we shall surely die."

Two contrasts between the natural world and the natural man are underlined by the apostle. Each we have already noted. Whilst the natural world longs for its redemption, the natural man is all oblivious of his only hope. He is blinded by the god of this world. He knows not the things that belong to his peace. Moreover – and we have hinted at this also – the natural world was not subjected to futility by choice, whereas the natural man deliberately seeks the way of evil. Nature was not corrupted through any fault of its own: it was involved in the fatal defection of Adam. But this curse upon nature, though arising out of man's sin, was imposed by the explicit sentence of God. Hence "him who subjected it" is not man or Adam or the devil, but God. However, nature is not shut up to despair, like the carnal man who glories in his shame. Even the word "subjected" carries with it a ray of hope unassociated with sinful humanity. In verse 7 of this chapter we learned that "the mind that is set on the flesh is hostile to God; it does not submit to God's law, indeed it cannot." Stern moral necessity prevents the flesh-mind from ever bowing to God's command. Apart from the Gospel, the unbeliever is subjected without hope. Not so the creation. Since it was not enslaved by its own will, God reserves a hope on its behalf.

The substance of that hope is contained in v.21. Bondage

will one day be ended by deliverance. Creation will be
set free from its shackles and gain an entrance into the
liberty and glory shared by God's children, "The redemption of mankind is also to be the redemption of
creation," comments Anders Nygren (alluding to the
new humanity in Christ). "For Paul the two go hand in
hand and are inseparably united. Just as God, on the day
of resurrection, will give man a body which corresponds
to the new aeon of glory, a 'spiritual body,' so He will
create a corresponding new cosmos, 'new heavens and a
new earth.' So the consummation will not come by any
automatic process of development. God does indeed lead
the whole creation on toward a goal which He has fixed
definitely; but the consummation will come through His
own mighty action; and it will concern not only individuals,
but it will have cosmic meaning and cosmic dimensions.
Only then, in union with this total fulfilment, will 'the
revealing of the sons of God' take place."

Glorified humanity and a glorified creation represent
the end God has in view. Scientific hypotheses which
deprive Him of that consummation must be tested by the
Word and will be disproved in the event. As Dr. C. Ryder
Smith reminds us, "the Future Kingdom glows with
glory," and the assurance of Scripture is that the world
will end neither with a bang nor a whimper, but with
an acclamation of Him who does all things well. The
passing of the earth that now is will make possible the
appearance of the new earth where righteousness dwells.
The deliverance will also be a delivery in which the order
of glory is brought to birth. It is significant that the passage
in Isaiah 66 which prophesies the new heaven and earth
is preceded by the analogy of labour-pains (Isa. 66:7–9;
22). These are anticipated even in this present age by the
natural world, struggling even now to be liberated from
its bondage, as we learn from the next couplet.

III. TRAVAIL AND REDEMPTION (vv.22,23). Paul is still
speaking about "the whole creation" or "sentient universe"

(A. S. Way). "We know" is explained by v.23: "we ourselves, who have the first fruits of the Spirit." This, then,
is not a matter of general knowledge, as if everyone was
aware of nature's pangs. That is plainly not so. Even the
scientists whose task it is to examine the phenomena of
the material universe, are unable to trace the evidence,
unless aided by revelation. This is something we know as
Christians, because God the Creator has told us in His
Word. The entire created order groans in all its parts as
if it were in the throes of childbirth – and indeed it is.
The verb for groan is *sustenazō* – "to sigh deeply, to wail."
Literally, it means "to contract or make narrow," from
stenos. A stenographer is not someone who groans at her
work (though that may sometimes be the case!) but
someone who takes down what is said in shorthand so
that it can be "narrowly written." There is, as Philippi
has put it, a great symphony of sighs arising from all
creation. "Multitudinous is the suppressed agonizing of
the whole creature world," comments Professor Lenski,
"under the distress which man's sin and death have brought
upon it. A million things are wrong, and all nature, and
especially animate nature, shows it." Tennyson's "nature
red in tooth and claw with ravin" is the reflection of this
basic dislocation.

Paul adds another verb which deepens the anguish of
the scene. Not only does the whole creation groan: it also
travails together. But distressing as this universal agony
may be, it is not in vain. Once again the element of hope
is interjected with respect to the natural order. This is
not fruitless pain and woe, but labour in childbirth. "When
a woman is in travail she has sorrow," said our Lord,
"because her hour has come; but when she is delivered
of her child, she no longer remembers the anguish, for
joy that a child is born into the world" (John 16:21).
The end is not death, but life.

The Old Testament is full of passages which speak
both of the travail and the redemption. "The fields are
laid waste, the ground *mourns*; because the grain is des-

troyed, the wine fails, the oil *languishes* . . . . The vine withers, the fig tree *languishes*. Pomegranate, palm and apple, all the trees of the field are withered; and gladness fails from the sons of men . . . . How the beasts *groan!* The herds of cattle are perplexed because there is no pasture for them; even the flocks of sheep are dismayed. Even the wild beasts *cry* to thee because the waterbrooks are dried up, and fire has devoured the pastures of the wilderness" (Joel 1:10,12,18,20). "How long will the land *mourn*, and the grass of every field wither? For the wickedness of those who dwell in it the beasts and birds are swept away, because men said, 'He will not see our latter end' " (Jer. 12:4). "They have made it a desolation; desolate, it *mourns* to me. The whole land is made desolate, but no man lays it to heart" (Jer. 12:11). "The land *mourns* and *languishes;* Lebanon is confounded and withers away; Sharon is like a desert; and Bashan and Carmel shake off their leaves" (Isa. 33:9). And here are the anticipations of rejoicing when earth shall keep her jubilee. "Make a *joyful noise* to the Lord, all the earth; break forth into *joyous song* and *sing praises*! Let the sea *roar* and all that fills it; the world and those who dwell in it! Let the floods *clap their hands*; let the hills *sing for joy* together before the Lord, for he comes to rule the earth" (Psa. 98:4, 7–9). "*Sing*, O heavens, for the Lord has done it; *shout*, O depths of the earth; break forth into *singing*, O mountains, O forest, and every tree in it! For the Lord has redeemed Jacob, and will be glorified in Israel" (Isa. 44:23). "*Sing* for joy O heavens, and *exult*, O earth; break forth, O mountains, into *singing*! For the Lord has comforted his people" (Isa. 49:13).

Paul has something further to add in v.23. It is not simply the created world that groans to be delivered. So do Christian believers. "Not only the creation, but we ourselves, who have the first fruits of the Spirit, groan inwardly." "But," or "moreover," indicates that the argument is being carried a stage further, in the statement that whilst the creation was subjected in hope (v.20),

believers actually possess the first fruits of the Spirit to
encourage them. Despite our inward sighs – inward and
therefore heartfelt and genuine – we are enabled to wait
in patience for our coming adoption, or, rather, the open
disclosure of our present adoption, of which the same Holy
Spirit even now assures us (vv.15,16). According to
Roman custom, adoption was twofold. First there was a
private transaction, which actually altered the status of
the person involved and made him the son of his new
father: then there was a public proclamation which
announced the fact to the world. The Christian is already
a son of God: but his standing will be manifest only at
the end when he is claimed by his Lord. The same eager
expectation which the creation displays (v.19) is found in
the believer as he fixes his gaze on things to come. He
turns from earthly preoccupations to await something
from beyond this mortal sphere. What he sets his hope on
originates in God's eternal world of joy.

The object of the believer's certain anticipation is the
declaration of his sonship through the redemption of the
body. When the body is raised from the tomb (v.11)
and joined in glorious rapture to the soul that has been
resting in Christ until the resurrection of the righteous,
then all that adoption includes will be made over to us
and manifest to all creation (v.19). The New English Bible
is misleading when it has "while we wait for God to make
us his sons and set our whole body free." We do not have
to wait for God to make us His sons: we can enjoy that
relationship now. But only at the end shall we enter into
the consummation and revelation of that sonship.

Redemption is one of the great Greek words of the New
Testament – *apolutrōsis*. It is one of three major terms
associated with the atonement wrought by our Lord on
the Cross. The other two are reconciliation and propitiation. *Apolutrōsis* is linked to another keyword: namely,
lutron (ransom) as used by our Lord in Mark 10:45. "For
the Son of man came not to be served but to serve, and to
give his life as a ransom for many." Redemption is a term

that has to do with the manumission of slaves. As Archbishop Trench pointed out, in his invaluable study of New Testament synonyms, it "is not recall from captivity merely, but recall from captivity through the payment of a ransom." Adolf Deissmann, in *Light from the Ancient East*, insisted that the conception of a price is not "a pictorial detail of no ulterior significance" but "a necessary link in the chain of thought." A ransom has been paid at Calvary not only covering our rescue from Satan and sin, but also the final deliverance of the body from mortality. When we sing of our Redeemer and praise Him for the death He died on our behalf, we should include this ultimate redemption in our catalogue of adoring gratitude.

IV. HOPE AND PATIENCE (vv.24,25). We cannot eliminate the reference to the last things from the vital core of the Gospel. Belief in the Lord's return and all that goes with it is not a kind of supplement to the faith that may be conveniently ignored by those who have no taste for such things. It is the very throbbing heart of our present confidence. "If Christianity be not altogether restless eschatology," declared Karl Barth characteristically, "there remains in it no relationship whatever to Christ."

The commentators discuss at considerable length how we should understand the dative in v.24. Is it "For we are saved *by* hope" (A.V.); "for *in* this hope we were saved" (R.S.V.); or "for *to* this hope we were saved"? Most modern translations seem to prefer "in," or "on the ground of." But there is much to be said for the last of the three possibilities, which takes the dative as relating to the indirect object. When we were saved, the apostle would then be telling us, it was to or for this hope; that is, in order that we might look forward to the final redemption of the body. "We have been saved from the sinking ship into the lifeboat," said Agar Beet, "but not yet into the haven." We shall be safe home in port only when in the glorified body we are for ever with the Lord.

It is of the very nature of hope that its evidence is

unseen. Hope and possession are incompatible. It is self-evident that we do not hope for what we already have. Once the hope is seen it ceases to be hope. Then, like faith, it is swallowed up in sight. Why should a man wait for what he can enjoy even now? But if our hope is a true hope – that is, if it is fixed on the unseen and as yet unrealized redemption of the body, then it has to be awaited with quiet, brave endurance.

It will be recognized that faith and hope are so closely allied as almost to be merged in these verses. But the distinctions are sufficiently clear elsewhere in Scripture. This is how Matthew Henry differentiates them: "Faith respects the promise: hope the thing promised. Faith is the evidence, hope the expectation of things not seen. Faith is the mother of hope." And John Trapp reaches a like conclusion when he affirms that "hope is the daughter of faith, but such as is a staff to her aged mother."

It is in this emphasis on hope that we discover the deepest incentive to holiness. It is the blessed anticipation of the Lord's coming for His own which lures us on to lead the life of the Spirit. We must, of course, covet it for its own sake and in obedience to God's command. But He graciously permits this shining expectation to bring us comfort and joy as we tread the heavenward way. "And every one who thus hopes in him purifies himself as he is pure" (I John 3:3). "Two things are commanded to the believer," according to Calvin; "to run with zest, and to keep the end in view." We shall be enabled to run with zest only if we do keep the end in view. The first fruits of the Spirit are given as a gracious foretaste of the powers of the age to come.

CHAPTER NINE

THE INTERCESSION OF THE SPIRIT

THE DOCTRINE OF THE TRINITY has been called the distinctive feature of Christianity. Certainly it is unique to the Gospel and fundamental to our faith. Yet, despite a general recognition of its basic importance, this teaching has not succeeded by and large in capturing the minds of believers and impressing them with its value for daily living. This is probably because we have somehow sealed off this truth from Christian experience. We have regarded it as an intellectual concept and overlooked the fact that, as the Savoy Conference put it, "the doctrine of the Trinity is the foundation of all our communion with God, and comfortable dependence upon Him."

In his autobiography *The Trodden Road* Dr. Albert Mansbridge shares the excitement of his discovery that this much misunderstood item of belief had a vital bearing upon his personal experience. "This is the Christian faith revealed to me by those who have borne witness to it, and responded to by me in the power of my own spirit. It is mysterious, but the doctrine of the Trinity in Unity of God meets the needs of human nature – God above, God incarnate, God inspiring. The whole being vibrates to its truth. Those who accept, or who are proceeding to the acceptance of its truth, are in the blessed company of all faithful people, and are immunized from capture by the spirits of evil – Satan and his angels – although they may be sore let and hindered, even injured, in their bodies and minds."

All too often we fail to realize the practical and experimental applications of this cardinal affirmation concerning

the Godhead. We mistakenly imagine that the idea of
the Trinity is merely a piece of gratuitous speculation
invented by the theologians who in their own sinister
interests wanted to complicate the simple Gospel of Jesus.
We forget that it is a firm revelation from God's Word and
that its purpose is not to confuse our minds but to fortify
our spirits. All that we enjoy in Christian experience comes
to us from the Father, in the Son and by the Spirit.

The closing verses of Romans Eight, from 26 to 39,
speak about the work of the Divine Trinity in believers,
as Dr. Dake brings out in his analysis. In verses 26 and
27, which are our immediate concern, the work of God the
Holy Spirit in the believer's life is described. In verses
28 to 33 the work of God the Father in the believer's
life is described. In verses 34 to 39 the work of God the
Son in the believer's life is described. In addition to the
more specific and explicit statements of Scripture relating
to the Holy Trinity – and they are more numerous than
the Jehovah's Witness on our doorstep would have us
believe – there are many more incidental corroborations
of the truth, of which this passage is but one example.

The usual order – Father, Son and Holy Ghost – is
adjusted here so as to highlight the operation of the Spirit
as applying to the believer's heart both the love of God
and the death of Christ. This is the sequence of Christian
experience, for although the unawakened sinner may not
be aware of the fact, it is the Holy Spirit who first makes
contact with his unregenerate heart and begins to bring
him to conviction, confession, repentance and faith.

But here it is the Spirit's influence on the redeemed
life that is under review and the apostle Paul deals in
these two verses with the intercession of the Spirit. Nowhere
else in the whole of Scripture are we told more about the
Spirit's relationship to prayer. We are given a glimpse
of His most intimate dealings with the human consciousness
and made indeed to feel that without His gracious aid we
could never pray at all. And that, of course, is the literal
truth. Apart from the cooperation of the Comforter there

can be no real prayer. The determinative factor is not our will. We cannot pray of ourselves any more than we can save or sanctify ourselves. The initiative and dynamic of prayer come from God the Father, through the Holy Spirit. As the Spirit occupies our lives, prayer becomes, as Dr. C. H. Dodd has it, "the Divine in us appealing to the God above us." Deep calls to deep: but both the depth within and the depth without is God.

These two verses tell us three things about the Holy Spirit and prayer: then those that follow (28–30) tell us one more. Together, they answer the questions When? How? Why? and What?

I.   WHEN THE SPIRIT HELPS (v.26a). It is "in our present limitations" (Phillips). Our need is constant and so is His aid. "Likewise the Spirit helps us in our weakness." Is that to be linked with the groans of creation in v.22 and of believers in v.23, since the Spirit also groans here in the latter part of v.26? Or is it not more likely that the tie-up is with the hope mentioned in vv.24 and 25, so that the sense is that just as our hope in Christ enables us to endure as seeing Him who is invisible, so the Spirit. in the same manner, supports us in our infirmities? The word translated "helps" is composite. He lays a hand on our weakness along with us and facing us. According to A. T. Robertson, it is "as if two men were carrying a log, one at each end." So the Holy Spirit takes hold of our incapacity and shares the load.

The particular weakness which the apostle has in mind is our ineffectiveness in prayer. That is *when* the Spirit helps. It is when we are feeble in the life of prayer that He equips us to be strong. When we cannot cope ourselves, He lives up to His name of Comforter and comes to cope for us. Our natural helplessness in the matter of prayer is presupposed. "We do not know how to pray as we ought" or "what it is right to pray for" (N.E.B. footnote). We are but vaguely conscious of our deep need: we cannot give it definition. And because we scarcely know what we want, or ought to want, we are unable to frame our prayers as we should. We stutter and stammer and feel that God cannot possibly make sense out of what we are trying to tell Him. Left to ourselves we neither know what prayer to offer nor how to offer it.

No doubt such a frank appraisal of the prayer situation strikes a responsive chord in our hearts. The realism of Scripture here appeals to us. If this is indeed how we feel about prayer, there is nothing unusual nor should we be unduly discouraged. We shall never make headway in the pilgrimage of prayer unless we begin by recognizing our human inability in this vital matter. Despite all that has been said and written about the naturalness of prayer and man as a praying animal, the truth of Scripture remains unassailable. "We do not know" – even Christians, let alone the unbeliever – "how to pray as we ought."

But there is hopefulness in this recognition of helplessness. It is precisely at this point that the Holy Spirit can begin His work. Only when we acknowledge that we cannot help ourselves can He come alongside to help us. He takes over where we give up. Our weakness is the best qualification we can have to receive His aid. Does not that encourage us? So often we suppose that we can be said to progress in prayer only when we are able to express ourselves with perfect clarity and in flawless phraseology. We envy those who have acquired a fluency in prayer. But unless that fluency is a gift of the Spirit, it will prove a hindrance rather than a help. And if it is a gift of the Spirit, it will have been born out of human infirmity. The first essential in prayer is a sense of incapacity and unworthiness before God.

In his penetrating book on prayer, Oscar Hallesby, the Norwegian Christian writer, says of helplessness: "This is unquestionably the first and the surest indication of a praying heart. As far as I can see, prayer has been ordained only for the helpless. It is the last resort of the helpless; indeed, the very last way out. We try everything before we finally resort to prayer. This is not only true of us

before our conversion. Prayer is our last resort also throughout our whole Christian life. I know very well that we offer
many and beautiful prayers, both privately and publicly,
without helplessness as the impelling power. But I am not
at all positive that this is prayer. Prayer and helplessness
are inseparable. Only he who is helpless can truly pray."

Read the Gospel accounts and it will discovered that
the only people whom Jesus was able to help were those
who had given up all hope of ever helping themselves. They
were desperate. Think of Zacchaeus: think of the woman
with the issue of blood: think of blind Bartimaeus. Their
prayers were answered, and yet they were scarcely coherent.
They had no language but a cry. Yet their desperate need
and unutterable yearning made their prayers effective.

Every mother knows what Paul meant. A little babe
cannot speak to you. He cannot formulate his petition
into words. But he can cry. And you know perfectly well
what that cry conveys. It is the acknowledgement of
complete dependence. It asks you to do what you know
to be best. Our truest prayer is a cry for help, an S.O.S.,
an admission that we are nothing and God is all. That is
the beginning of prayer.

At this point of our abject extremity the Holy Spirit
appears as our Intercessor and Advocate. The picture
conjured up here is that of a man in a state of collapse.
His strength is ebbing away and he sinks to the floor.
His back bends, his knees sag, his head drops. In a moment
he will be flat out. Then someone comes and lifts him up
and takes his weight. So the Holy Spirit helps us in our
weakness. Our extremity is His opportunity.

II. HOW THE SPIRIT PLEADS (v.26b). He Himself
intercedes for us "with sighs too deep for words." If we
are so unfortunate as to be involved in a court case and
have been wrongfully accused of some infringement, we
feel unable ourselves to plead our own cause, for we are
ignorant of legal terminology. We need a lawyer who can
plead for us in language that the judge can appreciate.

Scripture tells us that we have two such advocates constantly at our disposal. The Lord Jesus intercedes above at the right hand of power, and the Holy Spirit intercedes below in the sanctuary of the heart.

Christ is our Advocate on high,
Thou art our Advocate within.

How does the Holy Spirit thus plead for us? This verse tells us. He takes our inarticulate aspirations, our feeble faltering requests, and He so fills them with Himself that they become what we can never make them ourselves – prayers that rise up acceptable before God. The unutterable gushings of the soul are translated by the Intercessor Spirit into the language of heaven, so that the Father may hear, forgive and save. He interprets our infant prattle and ensures that it prevails with God. "The prayers of the Spirit," said George Matheson, "are the unuttered voices of the soul."

There is a lovely story that Bishop Winnington-Ingram often used to tell. It concerns a poor orphan boy who never learned to read and could write only the first few letters of the alphabet. After his parents had died, he was dragged up in an unfriendly world. Once he heard a minister say that if people would pray to God, no matter what for, God would send them help. That was something he never forgot. Some years later the boy went to work on a farm. One day he was sent out into a field to look after some sheep. He was having rather a hard time and reached the end of his patience. Then he recalled what the minister had said and determined that he, too, would pray to God. So down he knelt in the hedgeback. Someone going along the road heard his voice on the other side of the hedge. He stopped to see who was speaking, and found the lad on his knees saying, "A B C D E – A B C D E — A B C D E." "My boy," he enquired, "whatever are you doing?" The boy looked up and replied that he was praying. "Why, that is not praying: it is only repeating the alphabet." Then the boy confided to him that he did not know how to pray, but he thought that if he just named over the letters he knew, God would take them and put them into a prayer and answer his request.

How right that lad was! The prayers we do not know how to utter will be heard and met by God, because the Spirit interprets them and makes them intelligible in heaven. What a privilege it is to have the Holy Ghost as our personal Intercessor! We greatly value the prayer of Christian friends: "Brethren, pray for us," we beg in times of special need. There are those who trespass beyond the permission of God's Word and vainly seek the intervention of the saints. How much more powerful must be the never-ceasing intercession of the Holy Spirit! Already the Son is pleading His passion on the tree before the Father's throne: "he always lives to make intercession for them" (Heb. 7:25). And now we learn that not only the second but also the third person of the blessed Trinity engages Himself on our behalf: "the Spirit Himself intercedes for us." How favoured we are as believers when this twofold advocacy is exercised in our support!

III. WHY THE SPIRIT PREVAILS (v.27). These Spirit-inspired prayers can never fail of an answer because He "intercedes for the saints according to the will of God." The operative clause is the last. The Intercessor only asks for us the things that are within the plan of God. The Holy Spirit prays as did the Holy Son: Thy will be done. Our Lord Himself assured us that we could have whatever we asked for in His name. So often we forget that condition. Our prayers then become selfish. They are not in the Spirit, and therefore they are not answered. "You ask and do not receive," says James 4:3, "because you ask wrongly, to spend it on your passions." Prayer is not simply another means of gaining our own ends. If it does not align our will with God's, it is of no avail. Only the Holy Spirit can help us so to pray as to be sure of an answer. He intercedes "according to the will of God."

Here are some wise and helpful words of Samuel Chadwick, culled from his *The Path of Prayer*: "The Holy Spirit creates the conditions of prayer. We may ask amiss, not only in what we ask, but also in the reason for asking. He sanctifies desire and directs it into the will of God, so that we desire what God wills to give. That is how it comes to pass that if we delight ourselves in the Lord, we can be sure that He will give us the desires of our heart. We want what He wills. The Spirit brings to expression the unutterable things of the soul. His groanings are before our praying, and our prayers are born of His travail. In Him is the supply of life and desire, wisdom and faith, intercession and power. He quickens desire, purifies motive, inspires confidence, and assures faith."

The Spirit is able to intercede in the line of the Divine purpose – "for God's own people in God's own way" as the New English Bible has it – because He knows the mind of the Father. He is permitted to share the Divine secrets. But the first part of v.27 tells us that the reverse is also true. Not only does the Spirit know the mind of the Father: the Father knows the mind of the Spirit. "He who searches the hearts of men knows what is the mind of the Spirit."

All three persons of the Trinity participate in this search, but it is clearly the Father who is referred to here. David reminds Solomon his son in I Chronicles 28:9 that "the Lord searches all hearts, and understands every plan and thought," and in Jeremiah 17:10 we hear God declare: "I the Lord search the mind and try the heart, to give to every man according to his ways, according to the fruit of his doings." That is the heart-searching of the Father. But in Revelation 2:23 our glorified Saviour addresses the church at Thyatira and announces: "I am he who searches mind and heart, and I will give to each of you as your works deserve." That is the heart-searching of the Son. In I Corinthians 2:9,10 we learn that what eye has not seen nor ear heard nor heart conceived – what God has prepared for those who love Him – has been revealed through the Spirit, "for the Spirit searches everything, even the depths of God." That is the heart-searching of the Spirit. He penetrates not only the heart of man but the heart of God as well. The Spirit knows what is the mind of the Father and the Father knows what is the mind of the Spirit. It is out of this deep, mutual Divine inter-penetration that the prevalence of the Spirit's intercession proceeds, and on the same profound level it is ratified and validated.

IV. WHAT THE SPIRIT PROVIDES (v.28). The lessons learned from verses 26 and 27 lead up to the incomparable assurance of verse 28 that all things are worked together for good to those who love God and are called according to His purpose. This is made possible only through the Spirit. Verses 29 and 30 are a commentary on God's providential plan alluded to at the end of v.28.

"We know," says Paul. That is in contrast with "we do not know" in v.26, and arises from "he who searches the hearts of men knows" in v.27. *We* may not know: but *He* knows, and so we may know in Him. That is the sequence which explains the progression from "we do not know" in v.26 to "we know" in v.28. The Spirit brings assurance not only of sonship, as in v.16, but of security, as here.

> *But God has a few of us whom He whispers in the ear;*
> *The rest may reason, and welcome: 'tis we musicians know*

– so Browning in "Abt Vogler." Transposed into the key of Christian experience through the Holy Spirit, that represents an insight in line with the New Testament. But we know only because He knows. This is not intuition: it is revelation. Amid all life's perplexities even in this baffled and baffling nuclear era, we can quietly rest in the confidence that God orders all things well. "Behold, I go forward, but he is not there; and backward, but I cannot perceive him; on the left hand I seek him, but I cannot behold him: I turn to the right hand, but I cannot see him. But he knows the way that I take" (Job

23:8–10). We may not see, but by faith we can know, and that is enough.

This, then, is a tremendously strengthening verse. We should bind it to us every day. "There are two Scriptures which should fill the people of God with joy and consolation," wrote Robert Haldane. "The one is, 'The Lord God is a sun and shield; the Lord will give grace and glory; no good thing will He withold from them that love Him.' Psalm 84:11. The other is the passage before us, 'All things work together for good to them that love God, to them who are the called according to His purpose'." "If, then, God will withhold nothing that is good for us," he went on, "and will order and dispose of all things for good to us, what can be wanting to our absolute and complete security? How admirable is the providence of God, not only as all things are ordered by Him, but as He overrules whatever is most disordered, and turns to good things that in themselves are most pernicious. We admire His providence in the regularity of the seasons, of the course of the sun and stars; but this is not so wonderful as His bringing good out of evil in all the complicated acts and occurrences in the lives of men, and making even the power and malice of Satan, with the naturally destructive tendency of his works, to minister to the good of His children."

The Revised Standard Version preserves an important distinction in the Greek which the Authorized obscures by including "all things" both here in v.28 and also in v.32. There is a difference, and it is a vital one. In v.28 there is no article in the original: it is *panta* – all things. In v.32 there is an article preceding – *ta panta* – the all things. The Revised Standard Version distinguishes between them by having "everything" in v.28. The latter phrase – the all things – when introduced in Scripture invariably has to do with the things of God, the things of the Spirit, the things of Christ. "The all things" means those belonging to God Himself which are sealed inalienably to the called in the plan of salvation. "He who did not spare his own Son but gave him up for us all, will he not also give us (the) all things with him?" (v.32).

But here in v.28 the apostle is not referring to "the all things." We do not need to be told that the things of God conspire for our good. That is taken for granted. Our problem is with the things of this created though fallen world, where sin and death hold sway, where Satan is permitted to exercise his brief authority, and where misery and pain and sorrow and calamity are rife. The assurance of v.28 relates to these: *panta* (all things) – not simply *ta panta* (the all things) of the spiritual sphere – are so overruled by God that they combine to further the highest welfare of His children. Paul has already told the Corinthians: "For all things are yours, whether Paul or Apollos or Cephas or the world or life or death or the present or the future, all are yours; and you are Christ's; and Christ is God's" (I Cor. 3:21–23).

The New English Bible gives a rendering on the lines suggested by Dr. Dodd in his commentary on Romans. Picking up a hint from a variant reading (cited by N.E.B. in a footnote in the Library Edition), he claims that what Paul intended was "With those who love God, He" (or, according to the other reading, 'God') "cooperates in all respects for good." The New English Bible reflects that preference by translating: "in everything, as we know, he cooperates for good with those who love God." That is a little stronger than Moffatt's ineffective "we have his aid and interest in everything," but it still falls short of the mark. By reducing the meaning to that of mere cooperation, all that is distinctive in the verb is removed. The working together is not between God and those who love Him: it is between "all things." Obviously, they do not so harmonize of their own accord. They are made to do so. As Moulton and Milligan show in their *Vocabulary of the Greek Testament*, with parallels from Hellenistic writers, the verb here is transitive – "to cause, or make to work together." It is not voluntary cooperation that is in mind, but the authoritative over-riding of divergent and even antagonistic factors so that despite themselves they collaborate for the ultimate good of those who love God. And whether the subject be expressed or otherwise, either implicitly or explicitly it can be no other than God Himself. It is He who compels all things so to gear in with one another that the combined effect is to promote the well-being of the elect. In the varied circumstances of life, for the Christian every detail is controlled by God so that all conspire to this end. Actual experience confirms the truth of this tremendous affirmation. Again and again the most contradictory occurrences have been used by God to produce the most unlikely results. The testimony of Joseph has found its echo in many a soul: "As for you, you meant evil against me; but God meant it for good" (Gen. 50:20). This may not always be apparent at the time of crisis, yet in the outcome the Divine wisdom and sovereignty over events is vindicated.

Amidst his gathering misfortunes towards the end of his life, when ill-health dogged his steps and he was involved in the financial failure of his publisher, Sir Walter Scott could nevertheless record this courageous Christian determination in his diary: "But I will not let this unman me. Our hope, heavenly and earthly, is poorly anchored if the cable parts upon the stream. I believe in God, who can change evil into good: and I am confident that what befalls us is always ultimately for the best."

Verses 29 and 30 form a commentary on what is stated in v.28. Already those who love God have been designated as those "who are called according to his purpose." Now the apostle elaborates upon what is implied in such a title. He unrolls a fivefold succession of foreknowledge, predestination, election, justification and glorification. But he does so in a sonorous series of active verbs which describe the work of God in the soul of man. They "spring up one after the other as though they were so many milestones," wrote Bishop Kirk, "on a road along which the Christian is being carried by forces over which he has no control." We have been hearing how God superintends the natural order of "all things" so that they dovetail into His wise design. Now we are told that "the all things," namely, those that belong more directly to the realm of the Spirit, are incorporated into a perfect plan to bring about the final fulfilment of God's will with respect to His chosen.

The way in which these lofty themes are introduced makes it clear that they are to be viewed in the light of Christian experience. That is their true context. We must beware of an unduly rigid systematization of what is essentially a matter of Divine-human encounter. "The idea of election," according to Professor Rudolf Otto, "namely, the idea of being elected and predestined by God to *salvation* – crops up as a pure expression of the religious experience of grace." "Let us approach the subject in the simplicity in which Paul presents it," urges Lenski. "He wrote for simple Christians who also easily understood them. Back of our call is God's purpose of grace and salvation; only in accord with it are we called. Already in eternity God knew all the called, knew them in His love; and then He also destined them to be finally made like His Son. Amid our present trials this is comfort indeed. That is nothing to entangle us: that is a sermon that ought to be preached often."

We shall content ourselves before we close with underlining what is the purpose of this quintuple process. Although it is indicated after the second – that is, after predestination – it is in fact the goal of them all: "to be conformed to the image of his Son, in order that he might be the first-born among many brethren" (v.29). That is the aim of God's design. Said Matthew Henry in a memorable comment: "Holiness consists in our conformity to the image of Christ. This takes in the whole of sanctification, of which Christ is the great pattern and sampler. To be spirited as Christ was, to walk and live as Christ did, to bear our sufferings patiently as Christ did. Christ is the express image of His Father, and the saints are conformed to the image of Christ."

Such conformity is both a present experience and a

future expectation. Even now, in this "now time," as believers are filled with the Spirit, they may be transformed by the renewal of their mind. This is a glowing possibility of the holy life here below. "Look for it every day, every hour, every moment," advised Wesley. "Why not this hour, this moment? Certainly you may look for it now, if you believe it is by faith. Accept it by faith, accept it as you are, accept it now." Yet, although the gracious work may begin at any time, it must continue all the time. There is no once for all transformation. Moment by moment we must grow in the grace and the knowledge of our Lord and Saviour Jesus Christ. And we must constantly pursue the objective, for it is only as we walk in Christ that we can keep near Him and be made more like Him.

But, while a present and increasing experience, it is also a future expectation. The renewal of the mind is *now*: the redemption of the body is *then* (v.23). We shall only be completely conformed to the image of God's Son when we not only share His Spirit, but His glorious body. "We await a Saviour, the Lord Jesus Christ, who will change our lowly body to be like his glorious body, by the power which enables him even to subject all things to himself" (Phil. 3:21). Yet that final glorification is so certain in the counsel of God that Paul can speak of it in v.30 as having already happened. Until that day when the sons of God shall be revealed, let us strive by the help of the Intercessor Spirit to approach ever more closely to the likeness of our loving Lord. May the lines of Lavater's hymn be our unceasing prayer:

> *O Jesus Christ, grow Thou in me,*
> *And all things else recede:*
> *My heart be daily nearer Thee*
> *From sin be daily freed.*

> *More of Thy glory let me see,*
> *Thou Holy, Wise, and True!*
> *I would Thy living image be,*
> *In joy, and sorrow too.*

CHAPTER TEN

THE SUSTENANCE OF THE SPIRIT

IN THE INTRODUCTORY CHAPTER of these Bible studies
we recognized that the Eighth of Romans is really the
Everest of the entire epistle. Here Paul's loftiest letter
touches its peak-point. What precedes has led up to this.
What follows is a deduction from it, for, after the parenthesis on the position of Israel in 9–11, we move to the
practical exemplification of the Spirit-filled life from
Chapter Twelve onwards. This Pentecost of Romans,
then, is the climax of the whole book.

In the section from verse 31 to verse 39 we reach what
might be called the climax of the climax. This is the conclusion of the matter. This is the grand summing-up.
No wonder these familiar words are stamped on our
minds and hearts. No wonder their cadences ring in our
memories. No wonder we are stirred afresh every time
we read or hear them. Erasmus exclaimed, "What has
Cicero ever uttered more grandiloquently?" Even the
most impressive and persuasive oratory of the classical
period cannot match the inspired Word of God. Inspiration
is best evidenced by its end-product. When confronted
with a passage like this, we are compelled to acknowledge
that this is something more than the voice of man. Were
he never so eloquent and impassioned, Paul simply as
another rhetorician – even a Christian rhetorician – could
not have aspired to such a height as this. The Holy Spirit,
Himself the *theme* of this incomparable chapter, is also
its *inspirer*. His signature is writ large on every paragraph,
as indeed throughout the rest of Scripture.

The Spirit is not actually mentioned by name in these

130

culminating verses. As we have noticed, the passage from
verse 26 to the close of the chapter deals with the work
of the Divine Trinity in believers. Verses 26 and 27 have
spoken explicitly about the work of God the Holy Spirit.
Verses 28 to 33 speak about the work of God the Father
and verses 34 to 39 speak about the work of God the Son.
But although, of course, the three persons of the blessed
Trinity are separate and distinct, they represent one
undivided Godhead, and each co-inheres with the other.
Moreover, in the Divine economy it has been determined
that whilst all revelation shall be in the Son, all application
shall be through the Spirit. It is only by the medium of
the third person of the Trinity that the love of the Father
and the sacrifice of the Son are conveyed to the believer.
In a very real sense, then, even though the Spirit is not
referred to specifically in these final verses, His operation
is assumed. As we read of the wonderful provision God
has made for us, we may rightly ascribe it to the sustenance
of the Spirit.

In examining the Book of Acts, scholars isolate what are
known as the "we passages." Much of the narrative is
cast into the form of a report in the third person plural.
Concerning Paul and Barnabas and Timothy and Silas
and the rest, we are informed that "they" did this or went
there. But every now and then, "they" gives place to
"we." The first person plural takes over, and the inference
is that Luke himself, the author, was present. From verse
31 onwards in Romans Eight one of the great "we passages"
in Paul is offered to us. The chapter has begun with "those"
in v.1. "Me" occurs only in v.2. Verse 4 has "us;" but then
Paul reverts to "those." From verse 9 it is "you," although
"we" keeps bursting in (v.12,16,17 and especially 22–26).
There is an unusual "I" in verse 18. But after the great
declaration of verse 28 – "We know that God works all
things together for good to those who love Him" – the
apostle resumes a calculated and impressive objectivity
in verses 29 and 30, which deal with the involved themes
of predestination and election. His verbs are all in the

aorist – even with respect to glorification, where we might have expected a future – for he is contemplating the believer's calling and ultimate beatitude from the standpoint of God's own purpose, complete from all eternity. Hence it is not "us" but "those" and "whom" – that is, not merely Paul and his readers, and the Christians of the early Church, but all in every age from first to last who had been, were or would be included in the company of the redeemed. Every soul to be finally saved is comprised in this designation.

But in verse 31 Paul returns to his own day and his own circle. He addresses himself to the Church that then was, and as the Spirit applies the words to us today, they are directed to the Church that now is. This is the confidence we share with all the elect, but the emphasis is upon us and our enjoyment of it.

The clue to this portion is to be found in a series of pertinent questions. Let us pick them out. In v.31 Paul asks, "What then shall we say to this?" Then follow two more enquiries which relate to the believer's resources. In v.33 Paul asks, "Who shall bring any charge against God's elect?" and "Who is to condemn?" The statement that he adds (taking it to be such, and not a further question) relates, like the queries, to the believer's security. In v.35 Paul asks, "Who shall separate us from the love of Christ?" and what comes after relates to the believer's victory. This is the scheme under which we propose to expound this final section, remembering that the overall theme of the Eighth Chapter is "Life by the Spirit."

I.   First of all we consider THE RESOURCES OF THE SPIRIT-FILLED BELIEVER (vv.31,32). "What conclusion can we draw from all this?" enquires Paul, referring in particular to the central affirmation of the previous verses, but also in general to the drift of the entire chapter. In face of, in view of, confronted by these things, what are Christians to infer? Or it might be, as Phillips has it, "What is there left to say?" We certainly cannot stand and complain

that ours is a third-rate lot. Doubt and fear and mur-
muring are altogether out of place. We can only rejoice
in the sustenance of the Spirit.

"If God is for us, who is against us?" So Paul asks in
a further question. The Emperor Maximilian had that
text set in chequer-work on his dining table, so that he
might be reminded continually of his spiritual resources.
Every Christian should have it inscribed on the tablet
of his heart. The Greek is graphic here. No verb intervenes
as a copula or connecting link. The italics in the Authorized
Version indicate the omission. "If God for us, who against
us?" is how it reads. The assumption is not in doubt.
There is no uncertainty. God clearly is on our side. It
has been the aim of the epistle to show that God is our
ally if we will be His. The implication is not that no-one
will oppose us, but that it matters not a rap who does.
Their antagonism cannot affect our status nor deprive
us of our resources in God Himself. They cannot be
effectively against us, for since they are enemies of God
they cannot hope to succeed. One plus God is always
sufficient to ensure a majority. "With the Lord on my
side I do not fear. What can man do to me?" (Psa. 118:6).

When the servant of Elisha counted the army sent by
the Syrian king to Dothan to apprehend the prophet,
he cried out in despair, "Alas, my master! What shall we
do?" But Elisha answered, "Fear not, for those who are
with us are *more* than those who are with them" (II Kings
6:15,16). And when the young man's eyes were opened
after Elisha's prayer, he saw that the mountain was full
of horses and chariots of fire round about the prophet.
When Sennacherib of Assyria invaded Judah and set
siege to Jerusalem, Hezekiah encouraged his officers in
these words: "Be strong and of good courage. Do not be
afraid or dismayed before the king of Assyria and all the
horde that is with him; for there is one *greater* with us
than with him. With him is an arm of flesh; but with us
is the Lord our God, to help us and to fight our battles"
(II Chron. 32:7,8).

That is the testimony of Paul himself. "At my first defence no one took my part; all deserted me. But the Lord stood by me and gave strength to proclaim the word fully, that all the Gentiles might hear it. So I was rescued from the lion's mouth" (II Tim. 4:16,17). That is what counts. That is what conquers. Since God is on our side, what does it matter who ranges himself against us? In Christ, as Paul is to say in v.37, we are more than overcomers.

> *Though the sons of night blaspheme,*
> *More there are with us than them;*
> *God with us, we cannot fear;*
> *Fear, ye fiends, for Christ is here!*

This same, sufficient God, who is the believer's refuge and ally, also supplies the resources of the Spirit-filled life. He will freely give us all things. "The all things" is the strict connotation, as is indicated by the article. This is the expression which, as we have seen, refers to everything God has and is. These He graciously undertakes to make over to us in Christ. "And God is able to provide you with every blessing in abundance, so that you may always have enough of everything and may provide in abundance for every good work" (II Cor. 9:8). Such is the prodigality of the Divine provision. We not only have all we need. We have more than all we need.

That is what Paul strains to tell us at the end of Ephesians Three. He reaches the limit of language. He comes to the point where words fail. One expression is piled on top of another, like Pelion on Ossa, but still the half cannot be told. He begins with the basic assertion that God is *able*. Then he says that this ability is not merely potential but actual: God is "able to *do*." Next he says that God is able to do *all* that we ask. Then he proceeds to declare that God is able to do *more* than all we can ask. Our boldest requests fall short of His readiness to respond. But God is able to do more than all not only that we can *ask*, but that we can even *think*. The measure of man's mind when stretched to the utmost of its capacity is unable to conceive what God prepares for those who love Him. But Paul has not exhausted the theme. God is able to do more *abundantly* than all we ask or think. There is a Divine profusion about the provision. Yet even that is not all. Bracing himself for a final assault on this summit of God's goodness and mercy, the apostle announces that God is able to do *far* more abundantly than all we ask or think. And that all these superabundant resources are available to us in the Holy Spirit is made clear here in Ephesians 3:20 by the phrase that follows in the original text, though it is made to precede in the Revised Standard Version, no doubt for emphasis: "by the power at work within us."

This liberal distribution of spiritual largesse is sealed to us in Christ. The gift of His Son is at once the measure and the guarantee of God's continuing supply. If we are in any sort of doubt as to whether God will in fact bestow His blessings upon us, or as to their extent and value – we have only to gaze at the cross: "He who did not *spare* his own Son" (v.32). The same word occurs in the Septuagint of Genesis 22:16 with reference to the willingness of Abraham to offer up Isaac. After the angel of the Lord – His messenger, whom we take to be none other than Christ Himself as being the immediate revelation of the Father even prior to the Incarnation – had stayed Abraham's hand before the knife-blow fell, he called from heaven a second time and said, "By myself I have sworn, says the Lord, because you have done this, and have not *withheld* your son, your only son, I will indeed bless you, and I will multiply your descendants as the stars of heaven and as the sand which is on the seashore. And your descendants shall possess the gate of their enemies, and by your descendants shall all the nations of the earth bless themselves, because you have obeyed my voice" (Gen. 22:15–18). As Abraham did not spare, or withhold, his only son, so neither did God. And as blessing to Israel flowed from the first sacrifice, so transcendently blessing to all the ransomed Church of God flows from the second.

This, then, is the proof that God is for us. "For God *so* loved the world" – that is, in such a *way* (not, "so *much*," as N.E.B.) – "that he gave his only Son, that whoever believes in him should not perish but have eternal life" (John 3:16). "But God shows his love for us in that while we were yet sinners Christ died for us" (Rom. 5:8). "In this the love of God was made manifest among us, that God sent His only Son into the world, so that we might live through him. In this is love, not that we loved God but that he loved us and sent his Son to be the expiation for our sins" (I John 4:9,10. It is one of the weaknesses of R.S.V. that it reduces "propitiation" to "expiation" throughout).

The reference to the atoning death of our Lord is made even more explicit in Romans 8:32 by the second verb. "He who did not spare his own Son" – there is the negative: "but gave him up for us all" – there is the positive. He was handed over to be put to death. God surrendered Him to His enemies who plotted nothing short of His destruction. Here, the sacrifice is viewed from the Father's standpoint. He relinquished every claim upon His uniquely-begotten Son. But it must not be supposed that this involved any imposition upon the Son that He was unwilling to bear. Other verses of Scripture look at the matter from the Saviour's viewpoint and confirm this perfect correspondence between the Father's will and the Son's willingness. In Galatians 2:20 Paul speaks of "the Son of God who loved me and *gave* himself for me" (same verb). Titus 2:14 refers to our Saviour "Jesus Christ, who *gave* himself for us to redeem us from all iniquity and to purify for himself a people of his own who are zealous for good deeds." Our Lord Himself had supplied His own version of the atonement: "For the Son of man also came not to be served but to serve, and to *give* his life as a ransom for many" (Mark 10:45), and that is echoed in I Timothy 2:5,6 with its allusion to "one mediator between God and men, the man Christ Jesus, who *gave* himself as a ransom for all, the testimony to which was borne at the proper time." This same verb is constantly employed in the Gospels to describe Christ's deliverance into the hands of His enemies and to death.

All our resources, then, conveyed to us by the Spirit, are the outflow of the Father's love, sealed to us in the gift of the Son. That is the first affirmation of this final passage in Romans Eight.

II. The questions which follow next have to do with THE SECURITY OF THE SPIRIT-FILLED BELIEVER (vv.33,34). Verse 32 rests on God's being *for* us: verses 33 and 34 on someone being *against* us, initially at any rate. As in v.32, however, all opposition is shown to be of no avail when God defends.

The scene is obviously in a court room. The judge has taken his place on the bench. The learned counsel for the prosecution and defence are sitting in their silk. The witnesses have been subpoenaed to appear. The public pack the gallery. And there in the dock stands the prisoner, flanked by his guards. As we look more closely, we discover that the prisoner's face is a mirror in which each one of us sees none other than ourselves. We are the accused. We are on trial. It is our fate that is being decided.

But as the case is heard, there is a most unexpected intervention. Its nature can be indicated by a story that preachers often tell, for no-one who knows it could fail to realize its applicability to this context. It concerns that fine Christian industrialist, Frank Crossley. One day he was fulfilling his duties as a magistrate in a Manchester court. Amongst the numerous offenders brought before him was a Salvationist lassie whose only crime was that she had held an open-air Gospel meeting in one of the city streets. It was a sufficiently spacious site and no real inconvenience had been caused to passers-by. But the Army was in its infancy and the object of much obloquy from those who did not understand its aims. Some over-zealous constable had charged her with obstructing the traffic and the girl found herself facing the bench. But she defended herself bravely and seized the opportunity to witness for Christ. Then Frank Crossley did a most unusual thing. He left his seat, crossed the floor of the court and took his stand beside her in the dock. It was one of those gestures which spoke more eloquently than any words that lips could frame.

In that memorable intervention we can find a parable which at least begins to suggest, in an imperfect human fashion, what our Saviour Christ has done for us. The magistrate has become our advocate. He has even identified Himself with our plight, for He who knew no sin was made to be sin on our behalf. He left the seat of authority He occupied in heaven above and came down to earth that He might take our place in the dock. And because He has accepted our punishment He can justly plead our cause. Our offence is not a trifling infringement of some local bye-law. Ours are crimes of deepest dye. We have sinned against man and we have sinned against God. Legally, we have no hope of reprieve. But Christ Himself undertakes to conduct our case. And He will not be satisfied until He has secured a verdict of acquittal.

> *Arise, my soul arise,*
> *Shake off thy guilty fears;*
> *The bleeding Sacrifice*
> *In my behalf appears:*
> *Before the throne my Surety stands;*
> *My name is written on His hands.*

But this is only the beginning of surprises. As the Lord Jesus Christ begins to plead, the court empties. In a moment the entire scene is transformed. Ian MacPherson has brought this out most effectively in one of his stirring messages, to which we have been considerably indebted in presenting this vivid picture. "You look for the charge, but it is nowhere to be found. For 'Who shall lay anything to the charge of God's elect?' You search for the judge, but He is gone. For 'who is he that condemneth?' You seek for the jailer, but there *is* none. For 'who shall separate us from the love of Christ?' No charge: no judge: no jailer. In the absence of these the trial must perforce be terminated. The case just can't proceed!"

Now it is with the first two of these three astonishing developments that we are concerned in verses 33 and 34. There is no charge and no judge. "Who shall bring any charge against God's elect?" The accusation has been destroyed. It cannot be discovered. Paul tells the Colossians that God in Christ has "cancelled the bond which stood against us with its legal demands: this he set aside, nailing it to the cross." (Col. 2:14). It was usual for condemned criminals to carry with them to the place of execution a placard announcing the nature of their offence. If, as in the case of our Lord, death was to be by crucifixion and the prisoner was bearing his own cross, then a soldier would walk in front of him displaying his accusation for all to see. Then it would be posted above him as he hung on the gibbet. Now since our Lord was being punished not for His own sins but for those of the whole world, the accusation written above the cross was not His but ours. He took it to Calvary and obliterated it. That is why there is no charge.

Neither is there any judge. "It is God who justifies; who is to condemn?" It is the solemn office of the judge to pass sentence where guilt has been established. In a capital offence he will put on the black cap and condemn to death. But in this fantastic court room, where Jesus Christ pleads as our advocate, it is discovered that even the judge has disappeared. No sentence can be passed where no charge is brought. The case is quashed and the judge vacates his seat. "There is therefore now no condemnation for those who are in Christ Jesus," as Paul had declared in the opening words of this Pentecostal chapter. It is not that God acts arbitrarily in asserting His authority in the face of justice. Paul is not suggesting that, whatever may be the rights and wrongs of the case, no-one will dare to condemn if God acquits. The judge of all the earth will only do what is just. It is only on the ground of what

Christ has done on our behalf and in bearing our condemnation that the Father can exonerate us.

Four successive stages in the redemptive work of our
Lord are next enumerated. It is upon these that His
effective advocacy and hence the believer's security firmly
rest. (i) *His Crucifixion.* "It is Christ Jesus who died."
He died at Calvary. He suffered the death of the Cross.
It was no ordinary end. No man took His life from Him.
He gave it of Himself. His was an atoning, sacrificial,
substitutionary death. He died for us – on our behalf
and in our stead. This is how it comes about that there is
no charge and no judge. "Since, therefore, we are now
justified by his blood, much more shall we be saved by
him from the wrath of God" (Rom. 5:9).

(ii) *His Resurrection.* "Yes, who was raised from the
dead." Paul corrects himself, in a way. There is more
to it even than this, he seems to say. The apostle is not
thinking, of course, that the death of Christ in itself is
insufficient. That would be far from his mind. What he
means is that the Resurrection made evident what the
Cross had achieved. The all-sufficiency of the death was
attested and made available only through our Lord's
rising again. "For if while we were enemies we were
reconciled to God by the death of His Son, much more
now that we are reconciled, shall we be saved by his life"
(Rom. 5:10).

(iii) *His Ascension.* "Who is at the right hand of God."
This was why He was raised from the dead. He reascended
His native heaven. He took the highest station, which is
His by right. But there He also carried our human nature
as the guarantee that where He is, there shall His servants
be also. "When he had made purification for sins, he sat
down at the right hand of the Majesty on high" (Heb.
1:3). His session indicates the essential difference between
our Lord Jesus Christ and the Levitical priests. "And
every priest *stands* daily at his service, offering repeatedly
the same sacrifices, which can never take away sins.
But when Christ had offered for all time a single sacrifice,

He sat down at the right hand of God, then to wait until his enemies should be made a stool for his feet" (Heb. 10:11–13). The Levitical priests had never finished their work: it was still imperfect. They *stood* in token of continued service. Christ *sat*: His is a finished work in which "by a single offering he has perfected for all time those who are sanctified" (Heb. 10:14).

(iv) *His Intercession.* "Who indeed intercedes for us." That is the present ministry of our Lord. Added to the Spirit's intercession of v.26 is the Saviour's intercession here in v.34. It was for the purpose of perpetual intercession that Christ was raised from the dead and exalted to the place of honour and power. It is on the sole basis of His sacrificial death that He can effectively plead before His Father's face. "The former priests were many in number, because they were prevented by death from continuing in office; but he holds his priesthood permanently, because he continues for ever. Consequently he is able for all time to save those who draw near to God through him, since he always lives to make intercession for them" (Heb. 7:23–25). Is it realized that the very first benefit Christ obtained in His ministry of intercession was the effusion of the Holy Spirit? He had promised no less. "And I will pray the Father," He had assured His disciples in the days of His flesh, "and he will give you another Counsellor, to be with you for ever" (John 14:16). That was a prayer reserved until after the Ascension. "I *will* pray the Father" – and He did. It was His initial intercession, and Pentecost was the answer.

> *Our Advocate there*
> *By His blood and His prayer*
> *The gift hath obtained,*
> *For us He hath prayed, and the Comforter gained.*

In this fourfold progression of Christ's Crucifixion, Resurrection, Ascension and Intercession the believer's security is assured.

III.   The last question is in verse 35 and has to do with
THE VICTORY OF THE SPIRIT-FILLED BELIEVER. "Who shall
separate us from the love of Christ?" Paul enquires, and
concludes that in all the things that might appear to do
so "we are more than conquerors, through him who loved
us" (v.37). Reverting to the court scene in the previous
section, we now find that not only is there no charge and
no judge: there is no jailer either.

It is the responsibility of a jailer to separate the condemned criminal from his fellow men. He is marched
from the dock and driven off to prison. He is kept under
the strictest supervision. The guilty man must be parted
from society. But those who have the Lord Jesus Christ
for their advocate need fear no such confinement. No
accusation, no condemnation and no separation is involved
for them. "I am persuaded" cries the apostle (A.V.) – and
that is something more than being sure – "that *nothing*
will be able to separate us from the love of God in Christ
Jesus our Lord" (vv.38,39). And the comprehensiveness
of the catalogue set out in these two verses indicates that
he really means nothing.

Twice over in this culminating column of Romans
Eight Paul lists the factors which might militate against
such a confident claim as he has expressed. First, he produces an inventory with a question mark behind it.
"Shall tribulation, or distress, or persecution, or famine,
or nakedness, or peril, or sword?" (v.35). But then he
supplies an even fuller roll-call in vv.38 and 39 and pre-
faces it with the positive affirmation. Phillips captures
the unshakeable confidence implied in the verb, as well
as its precise mood, as he paraphrases these verses in a
splendid manner: "I have become absolutely convinced
that neither Death nor Life, neither messenger of heaven
nor monarch of earth, neither what happens today or
what may happen tomorrow, neither a power from on
high nor a power from below, nor anything else in God's
whole world has any power to separate us from the love
of God in Jesus Christ our Lord!"

Such a passage as this is really beyond comment. The best thing to do is to let it speak for itself. "There is no arguing with such a certainty," observes Dr. C. H. Dodd. "Either you simply don't believe it, or you receive it as the word of God." We shall content ourselves with noting that the ringing watchword of this final section is victory. Verse 37 sums it all up – "In all these things we are more than conquerors." We are over-overcomers. We keep on achieving the most decisive victory. We lead a life of continual triumph.

William the First of England bore a worthy title which history has handed down to us inseparably with his name. In 1066 William of Normandy, as he then was, pressed his claim to the Crown at the Battle of Hastings. Henceforward he was known not only as King of England, but even more impressively as William the Conqueror. That is a title every Christian is intended to bear. Yet so many are content to be just William. Victory is our privilege, yet we prefer to eke out a miserable spiritual existence at what Isaac Watts called a "poor, dying rate."

We must not overlook the means of conquest. It is "through him who loved us." It is in Christ and by the Holy Spirit. There is no other way. It is not by our own loyalty or resolution. And the tense is past – not suggesting that He loves us no longer, but reminding us that His love was manifested once for all on Calvary. The immovable foundation of the victory given by Christ to the believer is the atoning death of Christ. As His blood goes on cleansing us from all sin and as the Spirit keeps filling us with power, we shall be invincible. Our victory over sin and circumstance is proportioned by His victory for us then and in us now. The victorious life, according to Stanley Jones, who has written so helpfully about it, "is the life of Christ reigning victoriously in every portion of our being and in every one of our relationships." Nothing could be more comprehensive than that. But we can only have victory in all as He has control over all.

We shall do well, as we come to the conclusion of these

expositions in one of the red-letter chapters of Scripture, to measure the cost of this life by the Spirit which Romans Eight describes. The Cross is central in sanctification as it is in salvation. It is as we realize the price that has been paid to make possible not only our deliverance from sin, but our growth in grace, that we begin to esteem it as we should.

God loved the world of sinners lost
And ruined by the fall;
Salvation full at highest cost,
He offers free to all.

That is the entrance into the redeemed life in Christ. But here is the wealthy place into which He waits to lead us, where His love *for* us becomes His love *in* us.

Love brings the glorious fulness in,
And to His saints makes known
The blessed rest from inbred sin,
Through faith in Christ alone.

That is the Canaan promised to the believer. It is the realization of a Divine love which has already been perfectly revealed in Christ and which through the operation of the Spirit is expressed in us. It is our privilege not to be separated from the love of God in Christ Jesus our Lord. It is our responsibility to draw ever nearer to it, so that we may be moulded into the likeness of His Son.